ART OF THE HOLD

Published by Sneaker Invest © 2021 United States All rights reserved. No part of this book may be reproduced or modified in any form, including photocopying, recording, or by any information storage and retrieval system, without permission in writing from the publisher.

This publication is designed to provide general information regarding this subject matter covered. Because each factual situation is different, specific strategies should be tailored to the particular circumstance. For this reason, the reader is advised to consult with his or her own advisor regarding the individual's situation.

The author has taken reasonable precautions in the preparation of this book and believes the facts presented in the book are accurate as of the date it was written. However, neither the author nor the publisher assume any responsibility for any errors or omissions. The author specifically disclaims any liability resulting from the use or application of the information contained in this book, and the information is not intended to serve as financial or other professional advice related to the individual situations.

This book is best used not only to build a lasting foundation but to serve as a resource you can turn back to. As a result, I would encourage you to hold on to this book, even after your first read. Read it as many times as you can and use the information as a guide until you feel like you are confident in your own intuition.

—Sneaker Invest

ART OF THE HOLD

Sneaker
Invest

Your subconscious is the gateway to your success. Only 5% of our cognitive activities are conscious—the remaining 95% are all subconscious. This includes emotions, behavior, actions, and most importantly for us, decisions. In the simplest form, unconscious behavior includes breathing, walking, and talking. We don't deliberately tell ourselves to take each breath, to lift up our leg, to move our lips—we perform these actions without thinking. On the next level, we have things like understanding a text, tying a shoe, or solving an equation. We can perform these types of actions because we have practiced, studied, and learned them so well that it has become automatic. This type of response can be developed for anything you choose. Through learned intuition, which comes from constant repetition (practicing, studying, learning), you can begin to rely on your instinct. This instinct will eventually become the product of the time you put in.

CONTENTS

CHAPTER 1	The Art of the Hold	1
CHAPTER 2	Introduction	5
CHAPTER 3	Before Investing	9
CHAPTER 4	Which Shoes to Hold	13
CHAPTER 5	Which Shoes Not to Hold	87
CHAPTER 6	When to Buy-in	107
CHAPTER 7	Bulk Buying	113
CHAPTER 8	How Long to Hold	129
CHAPTER 9	Selling	133
CHAPTER 10	Reinvesting	137
CHAPTER 11	Logistics	139
CHAPTER 12	Conclusion	145

CHAPTER 1

THE ART OF THE HOLD

Welcome.

Before you start reading, I would like to share some of my personal applications of the methods used in this book—not in an attempt to "show-off," but as proof and validation of this book's teachings.

In 2018 I purchased 55 pairs of "Cactus Jack" Jordan 4's. I paid an average of $400 per pair, giving me a total investment cost of $22,000. At the time, I had around $30,000 in my bank account, meaning I was putting nearly 75% of my available capital into this hold. And while to many this would seem too risky, or just a terrible idea, I trusted myself and my intuition. And I was willing to back up my confidence with my money. Six months later, all sizes were sitting at around $1,000 per pair, giving me an average profit of $600 for each shoe. This meant my $22,000 investment had turned into $55,000, leaving me with $33,000 in profit.

That's a 150% return on my investment, in just six months. To give you some perspective, the average annual return on the S&P 500 is 8%. And while I'm not discrediting the validity of consistent investing in something like an index fund, the return on investments do not compare.

That same year, I purchased 21 pairs of the Jordan 1 x Off-White "UNC." I paid an average of $700 for sizes ranging from 6–13, giving me a total investment cost of $14,700. Again, to many this would seem like a risky idea. But again, I trusted myself. Eight months later, all sizes were selling for an average of $1,700, giving me an average profit of $1,000 per pair. My $14,700 investment turned into $35,700, leaving me with $21,000 in profit. That's a 142% return on investment. Again, for perspective, buying Microsoft stock would have given you a 41% return that year, which was one of the stronger investments in the stock market that year.

More recently, I invested into the Jordan 1 "Obsidian." I purchased 100 pairs, paying $180 for grade school sizes and $270 for men's, giving me a total investment cost of $22,000. Just five months later, I was clearing an average of $500 per pair, giving me a total profit of $28,000. That's a 127% increase—all from this book's methods.

To offer an example of a short-term investment, my $36,600 Jordan 1 "Mocha" hold gave me around $18,300 in profit after a mere three weeks. That's a 50% return in under one month.

I could go on and on with successful investments including the Jordan 1 "Shattered Backboard 3.0," the Jordan 11 "Concord," the Jordan 4 "White Cement" and many others.

The point of this book is not to share my success with you; the point is to share *how* I achieved this success. I want you to understand why I made the investments I did. Ultimately, I want you to be in a position where you can make your own investments and see the same success that I saw. I want you to have mastered the *art of the hold*.

CHAPTER 2

INTRODUCTION

There will always be people that doubt you. Your friends, your family, your teachers—they all have something to say. However, it's the belief in yourself that will lead to success.

    This trust in myself and my intuition made me over $500,000 by the age of 19.

• • •

October 23rd, 2015. That was the date I quit my regular job and promised myself I would never work for anyone other than myself again. I had been flipping shoes for a couple years at this point, and was starting to see some significant profits. Yet, my family never hesitated to remind me that selling sneakers was not sustainable. I remember a family member who would constantly bash what I was doing, explaining how I would be nothing if I continued selling shoes. My friends laughed when I told them I wanted to do sneakers full-time, leaving me to motivate myself. I was confused as to why they would pass up an opportunity to make money and angry that they didn't understand. But instead of taking it out on others, I used it as fuel. I needed to prove them wrong and was willing to put in the work to do so. Everybody around me told me that if I wanted to be successful, I had to do well in school, get into a good college, and then find a safe job. And while this way of life works for many, it wasn't for me. I knew that there was another way to reach success. I knew that sneakers were not "just a fad." I knew that if I applied myself to growing my knowledge and business, sneakers could take me places that good grades and a corporate job could never.

Six months after I quit my job, I invested into my first hold. I had been watching trends in the sneaker market for a while and felt ready to test my budding intuition. Seeing the past performance of the 2012 Jordan 4 "White Cement," I started looking into the new 2016 pair. After prices settled, I recognized that the sneaker was undervalued, meaning that there was room for growth and money to be made. I had begun to understand how much a shoe should be worth, and was able to compare that to the current market value. From 10 different sellers, I purchased 20 pairs of these Jordan 4's. I remember seeing the look of disappointment on my mother's face as I carried all the boxes upstairs into my room. Two weeks later, I brought in another 20 boxes, this time of a different shoe. My family kept telling me that I was wasting money, but, expecting a failed investment, they decided that this would help me learn that sneakers were not a sustainable source of income.

Introduction

I did learn from that first hold—but not what my parents expected. The Jordan 4 "White Cement" rose around $100 over the course of two months. I learned that I could trust what was the start of my intuition. I learned that to be successful investing in sneakers, I needed to really study the market—to gain experience through trial and error. I learned that if I had any chance of proving my parents wrong, of being my own boss, of making it in sneakers—I needed to master the *art of the hold.*

. . .

This book serves as a blueprint for prospective investors as well as guidance for experienced investors. I wish this type of information was accessible when I first started out. But I realized that because I had to learn on my own, I've developed a stronger intuition, and am in a better position to share my knowledge with others. I've compiled years worth of experience, trial and error, and hard work into this book.

The information you are about to read has changed my life. And I know it will change yours too.

CHAPTER 3

BEFORE INVESTING

Before investing your money into shoes, it is important that you understand what you are getting into. It's easy to see success on the internet and want to jump into investing right away. However, there are some things that you should know beforehand.

First of all, some shoes will be a long-term hold. You may not see a return on your investment for 4+ months to a year. If you aren't comfortable living without that money for prolonged periods of time, then maybe reconsider investing in sneakers. I typically only recommend investing into sneakers if you have at least 2.5k in available capital. If you're working with anything less than that, I would advise focusing more on "quick flips" (information on this in "How To Make A Fortune Selling Sneakers") until you've reached that 2.5k mark. While flipping shoes, you can practice investing in a couple pairs at a time to try to gain experience in the market. In general, when starting out, it's a good rule to invest a small amount at a time to minimize your risk. As you gain more experience and build your intuition, you can make larger investments. If you plan on investing a significant amount of money at the start, make sure to diversify your investments to limit the risk. Also, by diversifying your sneaker portfolio, you will be able to see which investments worked well, and which didn't. This method of diversification will help build your intuition.

DIVERSITY PORTFOLIO

Furthermore, as with any investment, there is a possibility that you will lose money. When starting out, it's beneficial to focus less on profit and more on gaining experience in the market. It's alright if not every hold yields significant returns off the bat. Make educated investments, but don't restrict yourself because you're afraid of losing money.

Once you understand what you're getting yourself into, it's important to recognize why holding sneakers can be profitable. In the simplest way, it all comes down to basic supply and demand. When Nike releases a Jordan 1 for a retail price of $170, they know they could charge more—but they place a higher value on building "hype" and exclusivity as to ensure people will come back for their next release. Thus, the retail price is lower than the price where the quantity supplied meets the quantity demanded (also known as equilibrium).

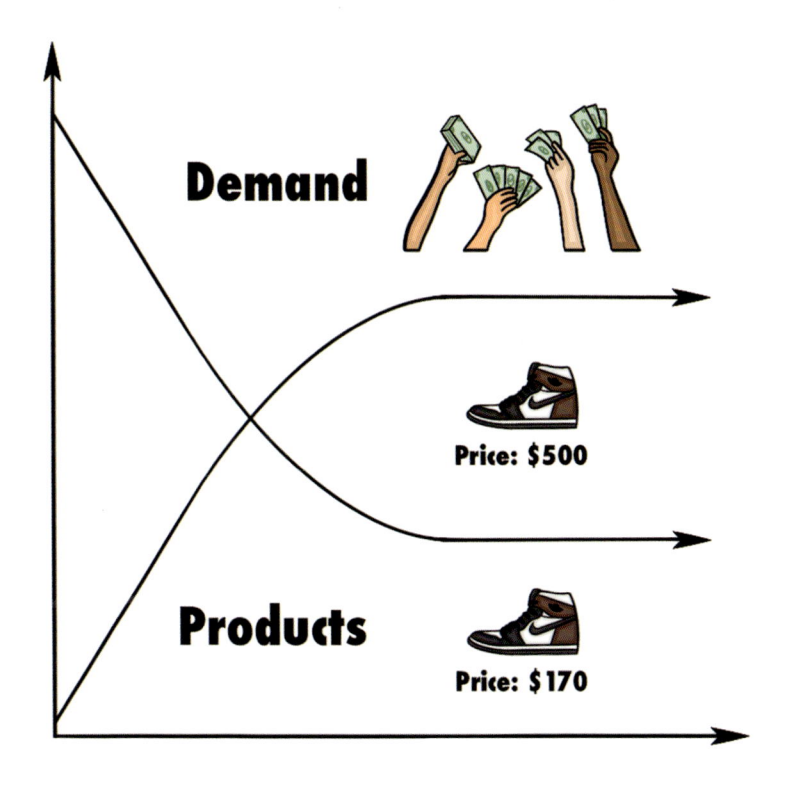

Demand
Price: $500

Products
Price: $170

Because of this, there is an aftermarket, where resellers can mark up their prices and make a profit. However, sometimes even after the aftermarket is established, the resale prices are still below this balanced point. This is what I am referring to when I describe a shoe as being "undervalued." The market will always move resale prices towards equilibrium, and we take advantage of this by investing into pairs. Of course, there are other factors that can affect the prices of a sneaker as well as shift the equilibrium price, which we will get into in the following chapters.

CHAPTER 4

WHICH SHOES TO HOLD

Affordability, Wearability, Visibility. These three factors, paired with past trends, can provide a strong indication of whether a shoe will increase in value or not. In this chapter, we'll look at these elements in depth and explain how you can decide which shoes are a good investment.

Affordability

This refers to the price point of the shoe relative to the number of buyers willing and able to buy the sneaker (demand at a given price). If a general release (GR) Jordan 1's resale price starts at $1,000, the average person who wears GR Jordan 1's will not be able to afford the shoes (think Smoke Greys or Royal Toes). However, if a highly exclusive Jordan 1's resale price starts out at $1,000, the average person who wears exclusive Jordan 1's will be willing and able to spend that much on a pair (think Dior's, Travis', or Off-Whites). So, "affordability" is relative to the type of sneaker and the typical group of buyers who wear them.

GENERAL RELEASE **LIMITED RELEASE**

To determine how much the average buyer is willing and able to pay for a specific shoe, we typically rely on past trends of similar models. For example, the Off-White Jordan 1 Chicago had a resale price of around $2,500 in June of 2018. At that same time, the resale price of the newly released Off-White Jordan 1 UNC was around $700. We can assume a similar consumer base for these shoes, and we can recognize that if people were willing to spend $2,500 on the Off-White Chicago 1s, then they would most likely be willing to spend more than $700 on the Off-White UNC 1s.

Which Shoes to Hold

OFF-WHITE 1 CHICAGO
Similar Shoes = Similar Results

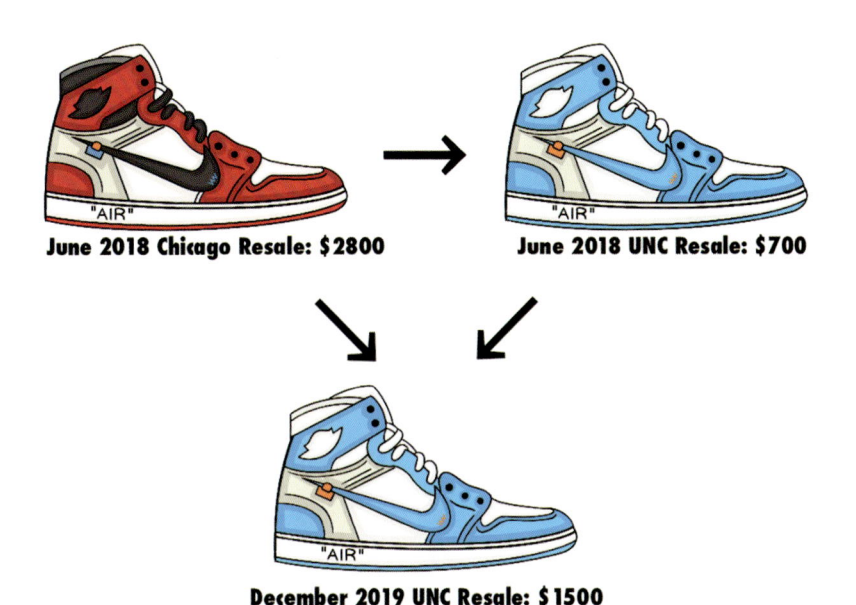

June 2018 Chicago Resale: $2800

June 2018 UNC Resale: $700

December 2019 UNC Resale: $1500

    This type of comparison can be used for most sneakers when looking at the affordability component and deciding how much people would be willing to pay for a certain model.

Wearability

This refers to the silhouette, colorway, and color blocking of the sneaker. Aside from a small group of die-hard collectors, people buy sneakers to solely wear them. Because the shoes we invest in aren't performance sneakers (e.g. running shoes, cleats or tennis shoes), they must have some sort of visual appeal for people to buy them. Occasionally, prospective sneaker investors will forget this key fact and dump their money into a shoe simply because they feel the prices are too low. If enough pairs are brought up by resellers, a "bubble" will be formed, where prices are high simply because there are not enough pairs available on the market. However, when these investors try to sell their pairs, they'll realize that the general public does not actually like the sneakers enough to sustain the high prices. Thus, the "bubble" pops and prices quickly drop as resellers get caught in an undercutting sell-off. "Bubbles" are easy to avoid if you make sure the sneaker meets the wearability and affordability standards.

While what's "in" is constantly changing, there are a few constants regarding which Jordan models and colorways are popular.

Jordan 1's, Jordan 3's, Jordan 4's, and Jordan 11's are consistently the most sought after Jordan silhouettes.

Of course, that doesn't mean that any colorway of these models will be a good investment—we still must consider the color scheme, as well as the other factors (affordability, visibility, and past trends). Still, it is important to watch how these specific silhouettes perform in the market.

As for colorways and color-blocking, there are some trends we can identify and use to predict demand. For the purpose of these examples, we will discuss the Jordan 1. The same type of analysis can be applied to other models.

The four original 1985 Jordan 1 color-blocking schemes I want to mention are the Chicago scheme, the Black Toe scheme, the UNC/Storm Blue scheme, and the Bred/Royal/Shadow scheme.

ART OF THE HOLD

Which Shoes to Hold

These four patterns are often an indication that a shoe will go up. Naturally, certain color schemes perform better than others, but we will cover this in our comparisons.

We'll start with the color-blocking of the Jordan 1 Chicago. We see the use of one color across the whole shoe (in this case red), with a neutral colored (black) on the Nike swoosh and top part of the shoe. We see this color scheme used in more recent releases such as the Jordan 1 Rookie of the Year, the Jordan 1 Reverse Shattered Backboard, the Jordan 1 Game Royal, and the Jordan 1 Court Purple 2.0.

CHICAGO 1 COMPARISON

ROTY

Reverse SBB

Game Royal

Court Purple

The Rookie of the Years have doubled in price since their release, the Reverse Shattered Backboards have tripled in price, the Game Royals have nearly tripled in price (after originally sitting at some stores and outlets) and the Court Purples have started to go up—but have not yet reached their full potential.

With the Jordan 1 Black Toe, we see the shoe sectioned off into two colors, as labeled below.

BLACK TOE COLOR BLOCKING

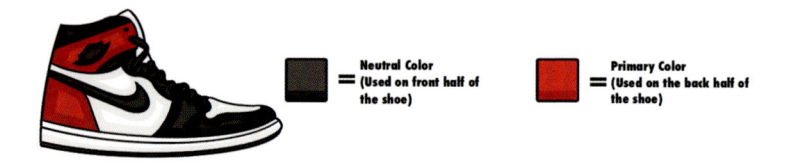

■ = **Neutral Color** (Used on front half of the shoe)

■ = **Primary Color** (Used on the back half of the shoe)

In a comparison that most people missed, we see the Jordan 1 Obsidian blocked off in the same way, with the UNC blue replacing the red, and Navy replacing the black.

BLACK TOE 1 COMPARISON

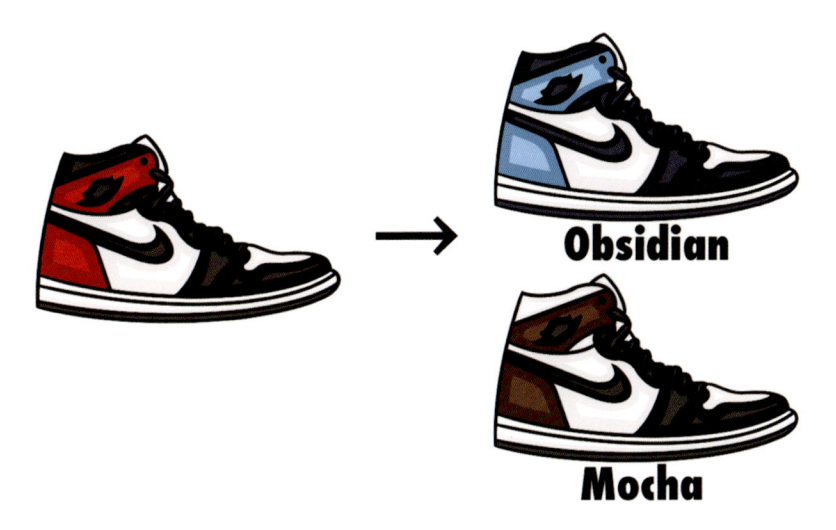

Obsidian

Mocha

The Jordan 1 Obsidian has doubled in price. In a more recent example, the Jordan 1 Mocha uses the same color blocking, only with a brown color replacing the red. This shoe has seen a 50% increase in under a month.

The Jordan 1 UNC color-scheme uses one color for all the accents on top of an all-white base. We see this color-blocking used in sneakers like the Jordan 1 Turbo Green, and the Jordan 1 Twist.

UNC 1 COMPARISON

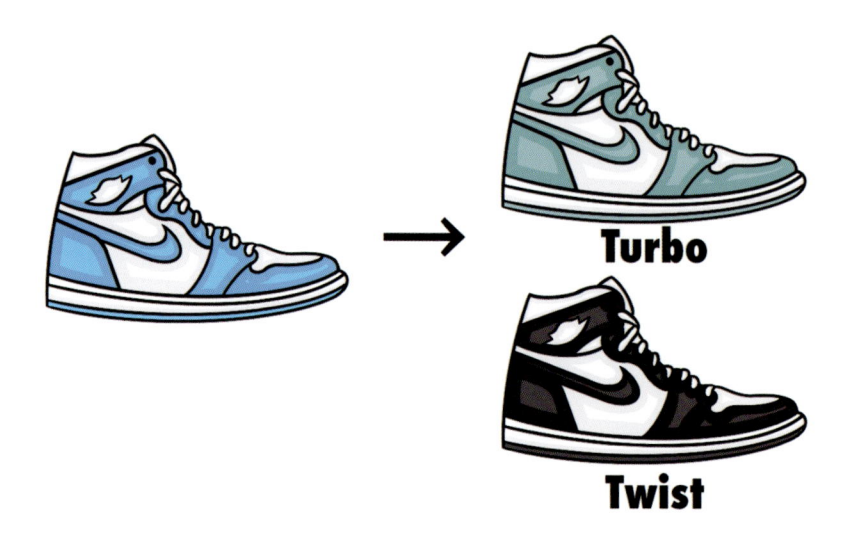

Turbo

Twist

    The Turbo Greens have doubled in price, and the Twists have tripled in price.

    The last original color-blocking scheme for Jordan 1's that I want to mention is the Bred scheme. We see a one color sectioned off with a black base and a white midsole. In the current market, sneakers with a lot of black on them are not as popular. However, we saw a strong comparison with the Jordan 1 Shattered Backboard 3.0. This shoe was ignored by many people because of its material—but, due to the similarities to the Bred 1, the Shattered Backboard 3.0's saw an increase of around $200 per pair. Current examples of this color-blocking include the Jordan 1 Pine Green 2.0, and the Jordan 1 Crimson Tint (which were once an outlet shoe).

BRED 1 COMPARISON

→ Reverse Shattered Backboard

Pine Green

Crimson Tint

    These sneakers have seen an increase in price of around $60 and $100 respectively, but not the exponential growth we see with other color schemes.

Visibility

This refers to who wears the shoes and who promotes them, which contributes to the "hype." If you've been involved with the sneaker game, you've probably heard a mention of the "Kanye effect," "Travis effect," "Kylie effect," and now, the most powerful, "Charli effect." Each of these "effects" refers to the incredible influence these figures have on what society deems "cool" at a given moment. The impact of public figures on the sneaker game dates to the 80's, when RUN-DMC released their track "My Adidas." When this song came out, it was unusual for athletic sneakers to be worn for style. However, as this song blew up, so did sales for adidas. In a pivotal moment in sneaker history, the group called upon their audience at Madison Square Garden to "hold up [their] sneakers."

Which Shoes to Hold

Thousands of people took off their adidas shoes and held them up in the air. An Adidas executive who witnessed this moment signed the group to an endorsement deal of $1 million—validating the impact celebrities could have on footwear.

In a recent example, when still signed with Nike, Kanye West wore the Jordan 1 "Bred" to a 2011 fashion week.

At this time, Jordan 1's had nowhere near the demand that they have today, and often were sitting on shelves, ending up unwanted and unsold. However, following Kanye's lead, Nike retroed the Jordan 1 "Bred" just two years later, marking the start of a run where Jordan 1s become arguably the most sought-after sneaker in the world. Kanye was the key to the growth in demand for the Jordan 1. Later, after switching to Adidas, Kanye performed at the 2015 Billboard Music Awards wearing the newly released "Triple White" Ultra boost 1.0.

Which Shoes to Hold

This sparked an incredible demand for the Ultra boost as well as other boost-containing products. Kanye is often credited for the run of success Adidas saw from 2015–2018 where Adidas sold millions of boost products including more Ultra boosts, NMDs, and Yeezys,

In 2020, we saw Kanye tweet a picture of himself wearing the Jordan 1 "Court Purple."

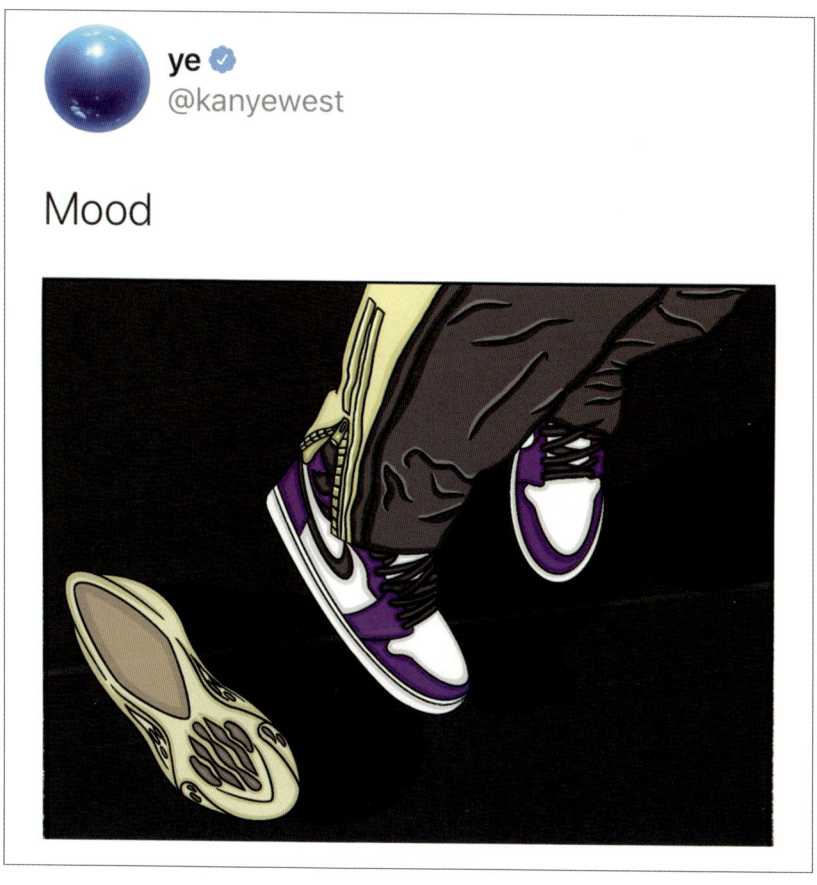

This single tweet led this sneaker to jump around $40 in value. Just from one tweet.

While on a slightly less-significant scale, Travis Scott and Kylie Jenner hold a similar influence on sneaker trends. Every picture, story and snapchat impacts the demand for the worn sneakers. And when Instagram was still the biggest player in social media marketing, Travis and Kylie were on top. But now, following the rise of a new platform where creators post short videos for the 800 million+ active users (more than Twitter and Snapchat), a 16-year-old girl has taken the crown for the biggest influencer on the internet. Charli D'Amelio boasts over 100 million followers on Tik-Tok as well as over 36 million followers on Instagram.

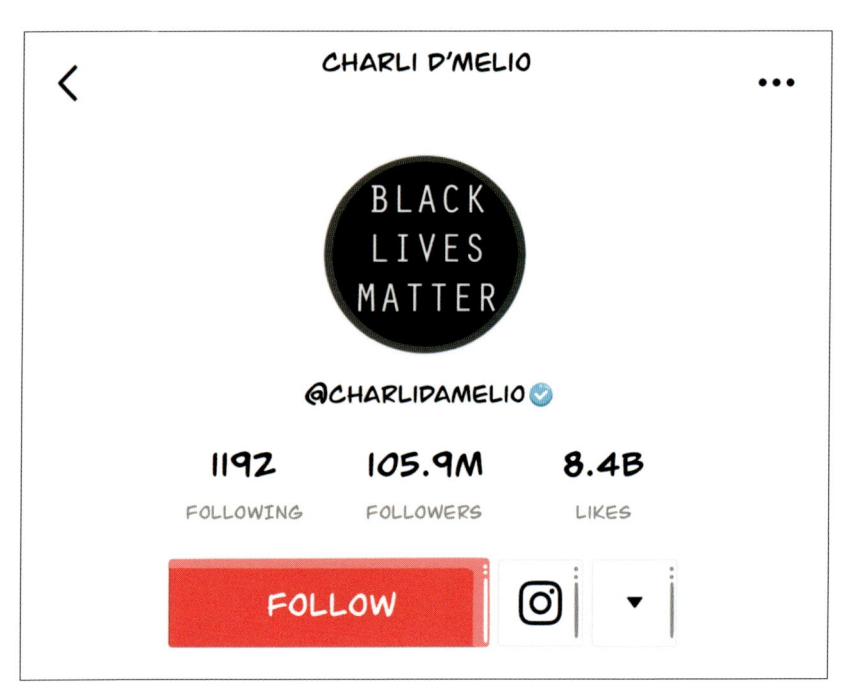

CHARLI D'MELIO		
BLACK LIVES MATTER		
@CHARLIDAMELIO		
1192	105.9M	8.4B
FOLLOWING	FOLLOWERS	LIKES
FOLLOW		

Her ability to showcase a product to millions of people at any given time is invaluable. She can dictate which pants are cool, which sweatshirts are "in," and most importantly to us, which shoes you should be wearing. And while we mentioned some of the other factors leading to the Jordan 1 "Obsidian" skyrocketing in price, Charli's impact was arguably the most influential. Oftentimes with our investments, we are confident that the shoe will rise in value, but the amount of visibility it receives will determine how quickly its prices increase. In the case of the Jordan 1 "Obsidian," Charli's followers started buying the shoe because of her, and then her followers' followers started buying the shoe because of them, and so on—until almost every social media user wanted to get their hands on a pair.

ART OF THE HOLD

charlidamelio

♡ ♀ ▷   ⊓

3,720,669 likes
charlidamelio 🖌 (mop)
photos by @bryant

The last example of visibility is the Michael Jordan documentary, "The Last Dance."

THE LAST DANCE

This 10-part series quickly became the most viewed ESPN documentary ever, reminding people of Michael Jordan's untouchable presence on and off the court. And like the saying goes, everybody wanted to "Be Like Mike." As people watched him lace up his Jordan 1 "Chicago's," they wanted a pair for themselves. Prices on the 2015 version of the Chicago's saw a staggering increase in price from around $800 per pair to $1800 per pair.

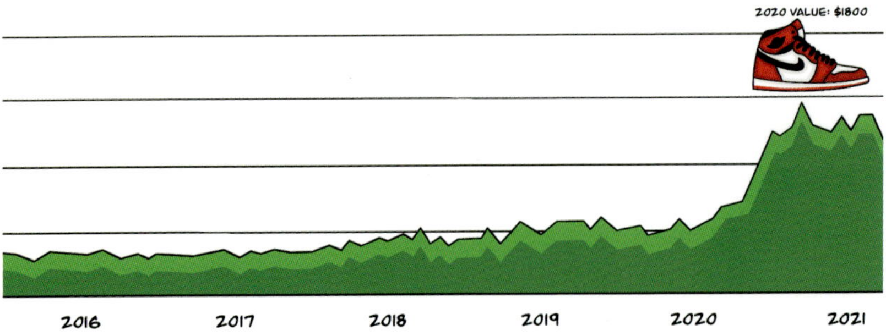

Not every Jordan shown in the documentary went up in value, however, so it's important to note that visibility alone doesn't cause a shoe to go up in value; it only speeds up the process. But if you buy-in to a sneaker that checks all the boxes for a good hold, and you know they will be seen, you'll find your investment to be extremely profitable in a relatively short amount of time.

Past Trends

History always repeats itself. Some investments are easier to identify due to a past release of the shoe that shows a strong trend. For example, iconic colorways and models such as the Jordan 11 "Bred," Jordan 11 "Concord," Jordan 4 "Bred," and Jordan 4 "White Cement" have all been released multiple times, each time performing similarly.

If you recognized this, you would have identified the prices of these models as undervalued after their most recent releases. The reason that prices started out so low was the high quantity of pairs on the market. An oversaturated market drives prices down initially—however, this does not mean a shoe can't go up in the future. The 2011 pair of Jordan 1 "Concord" and the 2012 pair of the Jordan 11 "Bred" both are valued at around $450. So, when the Concord's restocked in 2018 and prices settled to $240, it was clear that they had to go up. Similarly, when the Bred's restocked in 2019, they were available for close to retail ($220) and had nowhere to go but up. Now, the Concord 11's and Bred 11's sit at around $450 and $375 respectively. These "Classics" will always go up if the prices dip low enough.

Concord 11 Pattern

2011 Concord 11: $450 → 2018 Concord 11: $240

8 Months Later

$450

Bred 11 Pattern

2012 Bred 11: $450 → 2019 Bred 11: $240

8 Months Later

$375

Look out for future releases of the classic colorways, using previous releases as a guide. Expect history to repeat itself and expect pairs to perform similarly to how they did in the past.

Yeezys

Generally, I like to avoid investing in Yeezys because of the unpredictability of restocks and the general oversaturation of the 350 market. However, there are certain models that follow a similar trend, no matter how many times they get re-released—specifically, the Zebra 350's, Cream 350's, and Waverunner 700's.

For these shoes, because they've frequently restocked, it's critical that you understand when to buy-in and when to sell. The reason their market is strong is because they are some of the classic colorways that everybody thinks of when they hear "Yeezy." After the Turtle Doves, the Zebras are arguably the most recognized colorway in any Yeezy model. There will always be demand for recognized colorways, so they are typically a sound investment. Zebras have restocked 4 different times, each time following the same pattern: prices drop once the restock is announced and continue to dip until they are close to retail. This whole process of the prices dropping will generally take around 5 months.

After those five months are up, prices will begin to gradually increase back up to the $350–$400 range again. The Cream 350s follow a similar trend, dropping down to retail (even sitting in some sizes) for around 3–5 months after the restock before then starting to rise. The Waverunner 700s also follow this type of pattern except they start to rise in value sooner than the 350s. Waverunners will often start to go up after only two months of low prices.

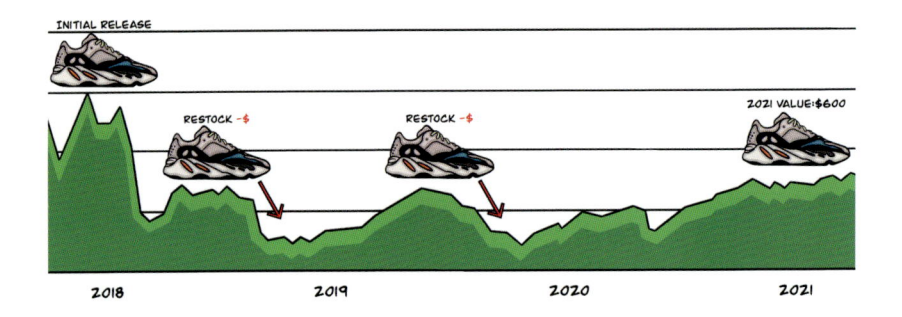

An example of another recognized colorway that recently restocked is the Bred 350. The moment the restock was announced, prices dropped from around $850 to $400—as they began to release in mass quantities, the Bred 350's dropped down to the $340 range and could follow a similar trend to the Zebras and Creams.

Kanye continues to put out new models—many of which are extremely unconventional. And while most people don't see them as very wearable, they tend to do well in terms of resale and investment potential. For example, the Yeezy Foam Runner Ararat, a shoe that resembles a croc, started out at around $250 and shot up to around $650 in the span of 6 months. Months later, Kanye dropped another colorway: the

Yeezy Foam Runner Sand. This new colorway is almost identical to the Ararat one, so we can expect people to look to the Sands as a cheaper alternative. Over time, prices should start to rise to come closer to where the Ararats are now, giving the Sand Foam Runners potential to hit $650.

YEEZY FOAM RUNNER PATTERN

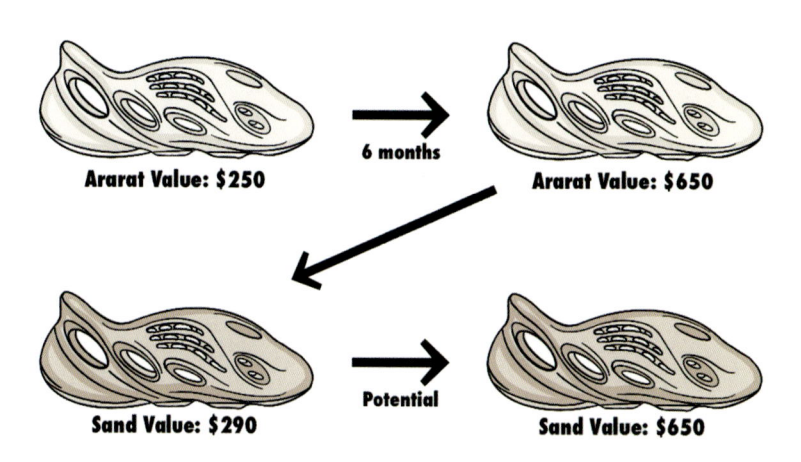

Ararat Value: $250 → (6 months) **Ararat Value: $650**

Sand Value: $290 → (Potential) **Sand Value: $650**

Another example is the Yeezy 700 V3 Azael, which started out at $450 and jumped to $750. Oftentimes these new models that Kanye releases are overlooked because of their perceived low wearability however you can ignore the wearability factor for the most part when he does release a new silhouette.

The oversaturation of non-classic 350 colorways has led their value to stay relatively low. They aren't recognizable colorways outside of the sneaker world, so non-sneakerheads will not be looking to buy them as much. As the Yeezy market continues to get flooded with new colorways,

I think that the demand will start to die down, providing little investment value besides some of the original colorways.

Look out for future restocks of the classic yeezy colorways—buy the dip and expect pairs to perform similarly to how they did in the past.

YEEZY SIZING GUIDE

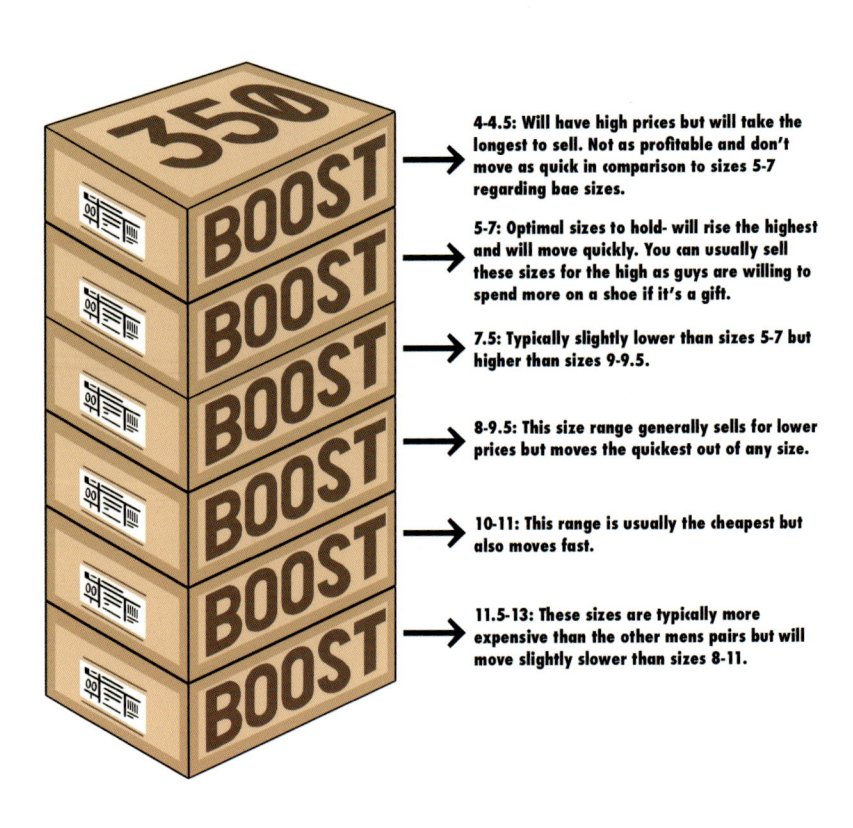

4-4.5: Will have high prices but will take the longest to sell. Not as profitable and don't move as quick in comparison to sizes 5-7 regarding bae sizes.

5-7: Optimal sizes to hold- will rise the highest and will move quickly. You can usually sell these sizes for the high as guys are willing to spend more on a shoe if it's a gift.

7.5: Typically slightly lower than sizes 5-7 but higher than sizes 9-9.5.

8-9.5: This size range generally sells for lower prices but moves the quickest out of any size.

10-11: This range is usually the cheapest but also moves fast.

11.5-13: These sizes are typically more expensive than the other mens pairs but will move slightly slower than sizes 8-11.

Nike Dunk Lows

Within the past couple years, the Nike Dunk Low has gone from sitting on shelves to the point where every colorway sells out. The model itself is iconic—originally released in 1985 in the colorways of all the top college basketball teams. It's always been one of the cleanest shoes and one of the easiest to wear. So, once they started to get a little hype behind them, it was no surprise that their resale prices took off.

In terms of investment potential, there is one specific color-blocking pattern that I want to point out. A white base with a single color on the Nike check and the area surrounding it, as well as the sole. Early 2020, we saw the release of both the Kentucky and Syracuse dunk lows.

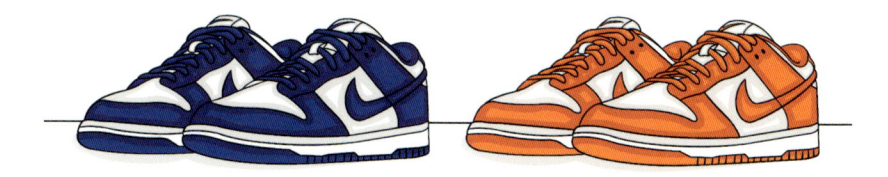

Prices started out in the low 200's and have since reached 600+. After people saw this dramatic increase, many thought that they could just hold any dunk low and expect similar returns. However, this is not the case. For colorways like the Champs dunk low and the Samba dunk low, prices have remained stagnant since release. It's important to focus on dunk lows that specifically follow the color blocking of the

Kentucky and Syracuse pairs. For example, we recently saw the release of the Panda dunk lows, which saw early prices in the low 200's and have since reached 300, with more room to go up. As I'm writing this, I just put $60,000 into 220 pairs of panda dunks in hopes that they hit $400+ long-term. Expect future dunk lows with this same color blocking to perform similarly, if prices start low enough (mid-low 200's).

While most people assume that this trend can be expected for high-top versions with this same color blocking, that is not the case. For example, the Michigan and Syracuse dunk highs have not moved much at all in terms of price since their release. This goes back to how the low top versions are simply easier to wear, so naturally there is more demand for them. In summary, stay away from high-top dunks, and stick to low tops with the Syracuse/Kentucky color blocking.

Jordan 1 Mid & Jordan 1 Low

In the past year, the Jordan 1 Mid has gone from one of the most disregarded models to one of the best-selling silhouettes. This is largely due to the increase in female "sneakerheads." However, these new "sneakerheads" are different—they place less emphasis on the history of the shoe and more emphasis on the style and who is wearing it. In addition, a Jordan 1 Mid is a much cheaper alternative to the high-top version. Thus, they do not care if the Jordan 1 Mid has been disliked in the past. As the number of these new buyers goes up, so do the prices on the shoes. As a result, Jordan 1 Mids (and Jordan 1 Lows) have started to see some of the strongest margins out of any investment. The average grade school Jordan 1 Mid retails at $90, meaning that it doesn't take much growth to provide high returns.

While many mids do rise in value, many see no growth at all, so it's not as simple as just buying a mid and holding onto it. First, it's important to understand how mids are released as it's not done the same way as a Jordan 1 high. Most mids are sent out to stores like Footlocker, Finish line, and Champs who will then put pairs on their shelves as long as Nike keeps sending them new pairs. There is not typically a set release date—the release usually happens over the course of a couple months. So, you generally won't see much growth if any during this time. However, after all pairs have been sold, a mid will almost always rise in value if it meets a couple main checks. To start, they must be selling in high volume. Because most mid colorways are mass produced, there must be enough people buying pairs in order to impact the market. You can check the number of daily sales on Stock X using the "View All Sales" feature. Generally, pairs that are selling well will have an initial resale price over retail. This initial price will often be in the $140–$160 range. Second, influencers must be buying and posting pairs. The audience who is buying and wearing mids is the most easily influenced group. If someone they follow wears a pair, the chances of them wanting a pair themselves goes up significantly. Finally, the colorway has to work well with what's popular at the time. A good example of this is the Jordan 1 Mid "Smoke Grey." At the time of their release, many girls were trying to match the aesthetic that came with the Jordan 1 High "Dior." Therefore, they turned to the very similar "Smoke Grey" colorway as a cheaper alternative.

SIMILAR AESTHETIC = SIMILAR PERFORMANCE

Dior

The key differences are the swoosh and the outsole

Smoke Grey

Prices on this pair have risen from around $130 per pair to around $350 per pair in 6 months. Another example is the Jordan 1 Mid "Pink Quartz" in GS sizes. This shoe initially sold in high volumes for around $130-$150. After finding its way into the closets of many social media influencers, this shoe has crept all the way up to $300 in all sizes. Again, this sneaker checked all the boxes: strong colorway (pink/white/black), strong initial value, and strong visibility, so it was bound to go up.

For Jordan 1 lows, many of the low top versions of popular Jordan 1 High colorways are strong investments. For example, the Jordan 1 Low Gold Toe, Royal Toe, Black Toe, Shattered Backboard, and Court Purple 1.0 all have high top versions that sell for over $300.

Thus, with initial prices of around $100, we could expect these low top versions to rise as people started to buy them as a cheaper alternative to the highs. More recently, we have seen a new trend start to form regarding a specific color blocking that I would compare to the Jordan 1 "Chicago." We have seen the Jordan 1 Low Gym Red, Smoke

Grey, Game Royal, and Court Purple 2.0 all follow the same pattern: starting out at around $130 and then rising around 4 months after their release. Future releases using the same color blocking should perform similarly.

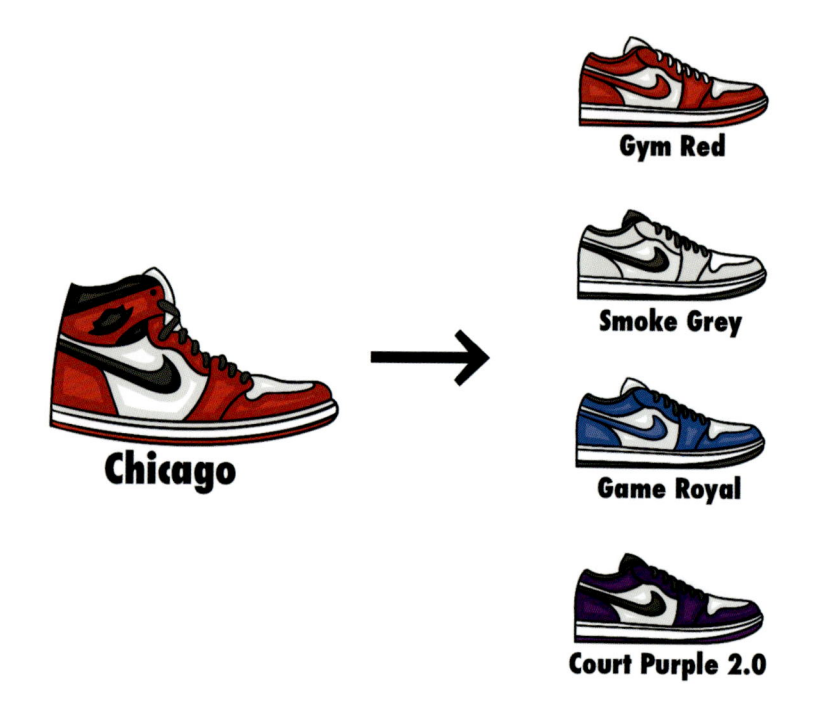

Jordan 3's

In the past, the Jordan 3 has seen very strong returns, mainly because of the low initial buy-in cost. I generally like to break up Jordan 3's into three main categories: classic colorways, pairs with White Cement 3 color blocking, and outlet pairs.

There are three main colorways of the Jordan 3 released in 1988: White Cement 3's, Black Cement 3's, and True Blue 3's.

These OG colorways always have had and always will have significant demand. Thus, we can expect rereleases to consistently hit similar prices to earlier pairs. For example, the Jordan 3 "White Cement" (with the Nike Air) released in both 2013 and 2018. Prices for the 2018 pair started out at around $280, and prices for the 2013 pair were around $500 at that same time.

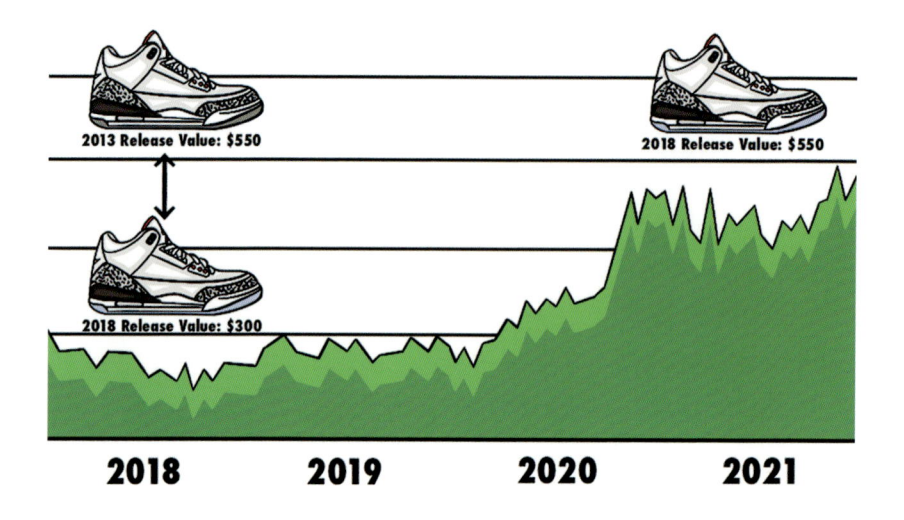

[Chart showing Jordan 3 sneaker prices from 2018 to 2021. 2013 Release Value: $550. 2018 Release Value: $550. 2018 Release Value: $300.]

So, we could expect the 2018 pair to reach similar prices of around $450–$550, which they did.

The Jordan 3 "Black Cement" released in 2011 and 2018. Prices for the 2018 pair started out at around $200, and prices for the 2011 pair were around $350 at the time. So, we could expect the 2018 pair to reach a similar price range, which they did. The Jordan 3 "True Blue" released in both 2016 and 2011. Prices for the 2016 pair started out at around $180 (even hitting many outlets), and prices for the 2011 pair were around $300 at the time. So, we could again expect prices to hit a similar price range, which, of course, they did.

Which Shoes to Hold

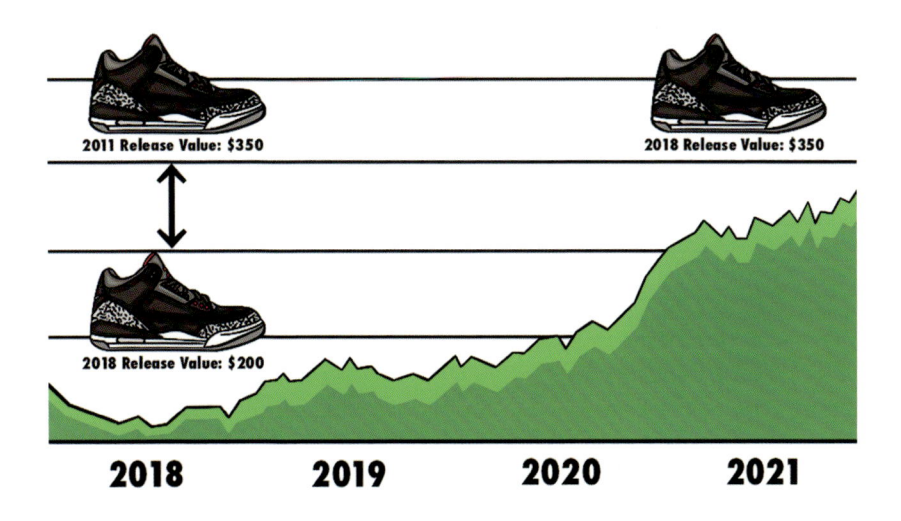

2011 Release Value: $350	2018 Release Value: $350
2018 Release Value: $200	

2018   **2019**   **2020**   **2021**

Arguably the most popular color blocking of the Jordan 3 is the blocking of the White Cement 3's. We see an all-white shoe with the classic elephant print and a flash of one color on the midsole (black for the White Cement 3's). Two examples that I want to point out are the Hall of Fame 3's and the more recent UNC 3's. The Hall of Fame 3's features the same color blocking as the White Cement 3's except with red replacing the black on the midsole as shown on the next page.

White Cement → **Hall of Fame**

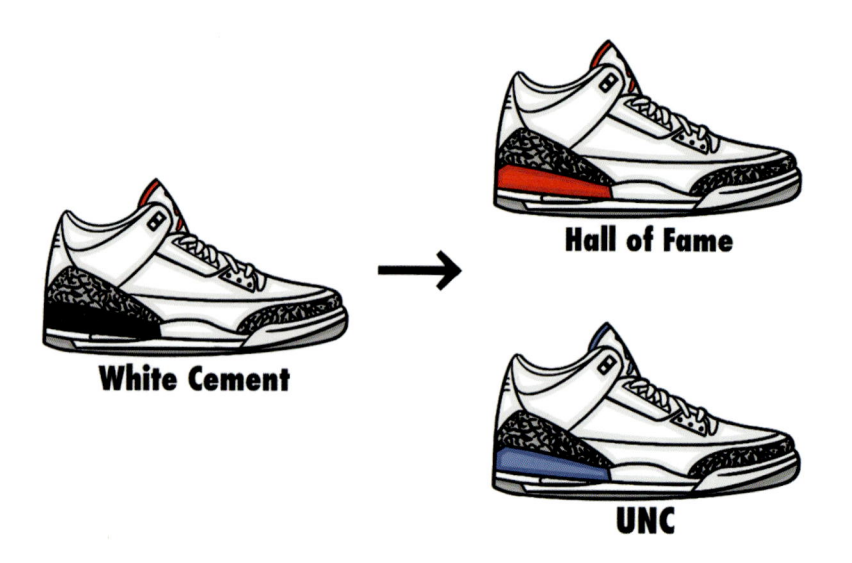

UNC

Prices started out at around $190 and have since reached the $300–$350 range. The Jordan 3 "UNC" also uses the White Cement color blocking except this time replacing the black on the midsole with a UNC blue. Prices on this pair started out at around $220 and are currently sitting at around $360.

The third category, outlet pairs, focuses entirely on affordability. If a Jordan 3 starts out at around $90–$110, prices will go up, regardless of wearability and visibility. Some examples worth mentioning include the Jordan 3 "Mocha," the Jordan 3 "Chlorophyll," and the Jordan 3 "International Flight."

Which Shoes to Hold

Each of these pairs started out significantly under retail and are now selling for upwards of $200. While outlet Jordan 3's do see significant returns, it does generally take upwards of a year to go up in value.

So, look out for future re-releases of the OG colorways, pairs that match the White Cement color blocking, and pairs that hit the outlets. All men's sizes perform similarly, so no need to focus on a specific size range when buying.

Jordan 4's

Around three years ago—before I started writing this book, people weren't really investing into grade school Jordan 1's. As you probably know, grade school Jordan 1's quickly became the most heavily invested in sneakers. We've seen a wave like none other, until now. We believe that grade school Jordan 4's will be the next wave. This "wave" is not an accident; it's been building for the past couple years. In the past two years we've seen Nike experiment with this silhouette—dropping two of what would become some of the most coveted Jordan 4's of all time: the Jordan 4 "Cactus Jack" and the Jordan 4 "Off-White."

As influencers continued to post pictures wearing these limited colorways, the demand from the masses started to rise. And while the majority cannot afford to spend $1,000+ on a pair of shoes, they are more than happy to spend $200, $300, or even $500 on a pair, especially when they can get a similar aesthetic to the more limited colorways.

As a result, we've seen incredible growth from general releases such as the Jordan 4 "Black Cat" and the Jordan 4 "Metallic Purple."

Which Shoes to Hold

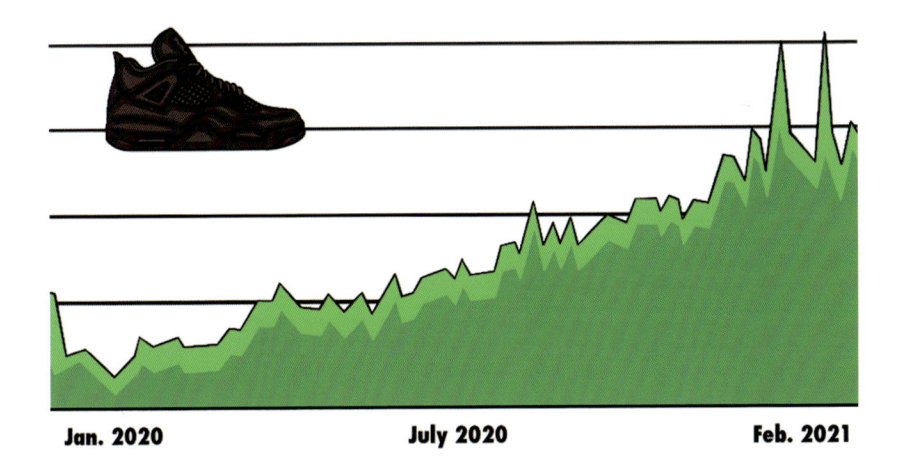

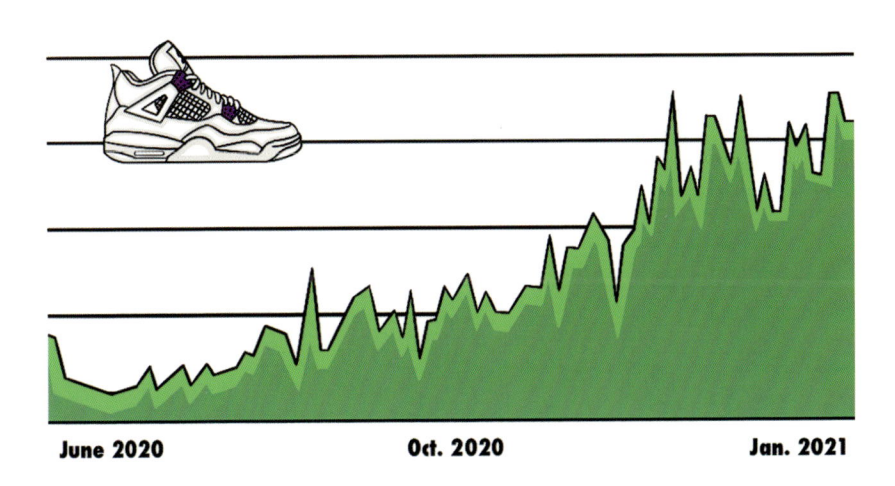

Jan. 2020   July 2020   Feb. 2021

June 2020   Oct. 2020   Jan. 2021

Even more recently, we've seen the Jordan 4 "Fire Red" GS (retail $150) go from sitting at most stores at retail to reselling for over $230 in under a month.

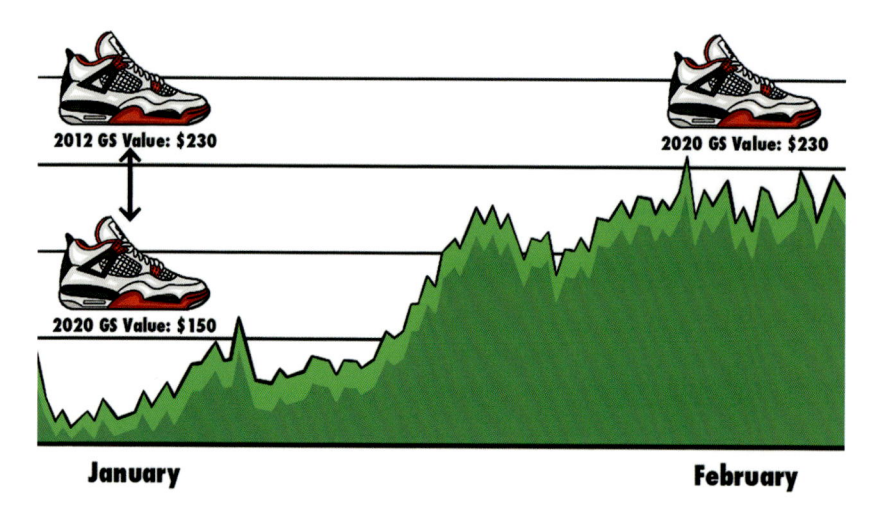

2012 GS Value: $230

2020 GS Value: $150

2020 GS Value: $230

January   **February**

As the demand for the silhouette increases and resellers start to catch on, I believe that the Jordan 4 will become a model that will always sell out, similar to how the Jordan 1 is now. And beyond selling out, I believe that the model, specifically in grade school sizes, will turn into one of the better investments out there, even beyond the 4's mentioned in *Past Trends* and *Outlet Holds.* Look for wearable colorways—whether that's neutral shades of white, black, and tan or brighter colors like university blue. Oftentimes you will be able to judge the hype and demand on the shoe even prior to the release by keeping a watch on what people are saying on social media as well as how many early pairs are being sold on platforms like Stock X. A Jordan 4 with a strong colorway and demand will almost always perform well over time.

JORDAN 4 GS SIZING GUIDE

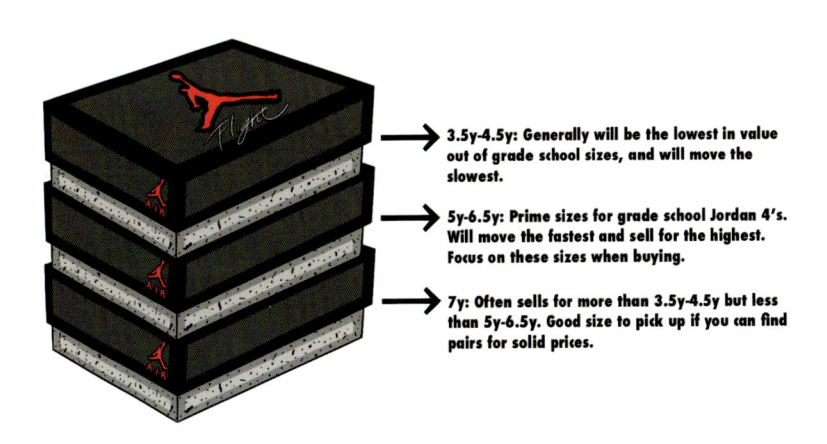

→ **3.5y-4.5y:** Generally will be the lowest in value out of grade school sizes, and will move the slowest.

→ **5y-6.5y:** Prime sizes for grade school Jordan 4's. Will move the fastest and sell for the highest. Focus on these sizes when buying.

→ **7y:** Often sells for more than 3.5y-4.5y but less than 5y-6.5y. Good size to pick up if you can find pairs for solid prices.

the Jordan 11 Closing Ceremony and Jordan 11 Cherry saw just around a $50 increase in value over the past couple of years. Some pairs that were stronger investments include the Jordan 11 Low Cool Grey and Jeter (both started out under retail and rose to around $300), Jordan 11 Low UNC and Infrared (both started out around $230 and rose to $350), and of course the Jordan 11 Low Concord, which started out at $230 and rose to $450. We can recognize that the Jordan 11 Low Cool Grey, Concord, and Jeter all have high-top versions that sell for over $400.

So, naturally the lows become a cheaper alternative that people will turn to.

For pairs like the UNCs, Barons, and Infrareds, it's more a result of general wearability with the Infrared and Barons having majority black/white colors and the UNCs having the iconic university blue/white colors.

In summary, for Jordan 11 highs, you can expect rereleases of the original colorways to always perform well. For other releases, look for pairs to hit around $220 before eventually rising to the $330 range. For grade school pairs, look for potential women's exclusive pairs, but also don't hesitate to invest into grade school sizing of regular releases. For Jordan 11 Lows, keep an eye out for pairs with classic and wearable colorways to perform well.

Jordan 12's

The Jordan 12 has historically been overvalued—oftentimes because of a collaboration. Similar to the Jordan 13, this is a shoe that needs to be bought-in at a low price in order to reach strong margins, unless it's one of the original colorways.

This necessity to be bought-in at a low price is best exhibited with the Jordan 12 "OVO" in black. A lot of people overestimated the influence of a Drake OVO collaboration—while Drake can and will help a sneaker, he can't impact the market of an all-black Jordan 12 with no reference to himself or OVO other than on the soles and the insoles (both not visible when being worn). Prices on this pair started out at around $500 and have since dropped all the way down to $320. Even an OVO collaboration could not carry a Jordan 12 when the prices started out high.

Which Shoes to Hold

In contrast, when pairs start out low enough ($170–$190 range), there is generally room to make a decent profit—but it still can take upwards of a year for there to be any movement. For example, the Jordan 12 "Dark Grey" started out at $175 and rose to $260. Both the Jordan 12 "College Navy" and the Jordan 12 "Fiba" started at $190 and eventually hit $270.

For the original and more recognized colorways, there will always be demand. Specifically, the Jordan 12 Taxis, Obsidians, Flu Games, Playoffs and French Blues have historically seen significant price increases following a more recent re-release.

The 2013 Jordan 12 Taxis started out at around $300 and are now selling for just under $600.

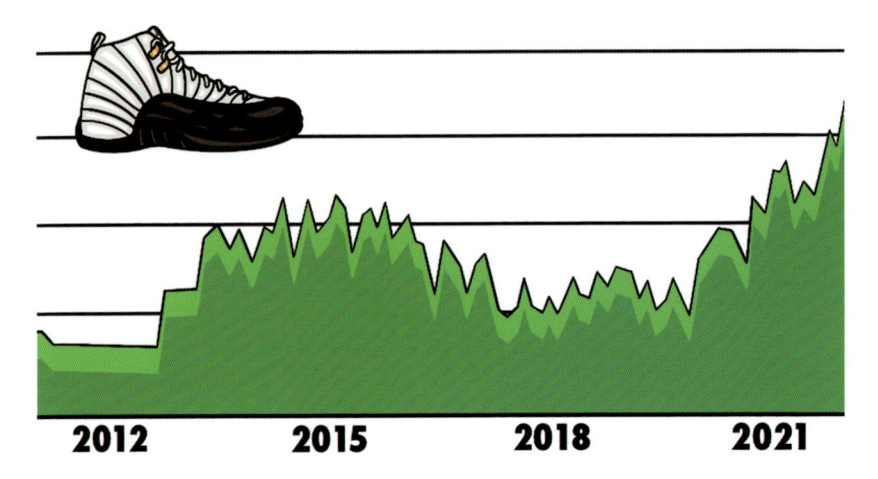

The 2012 Obsidian 12s were originally selling for around $180 and are now at $300.

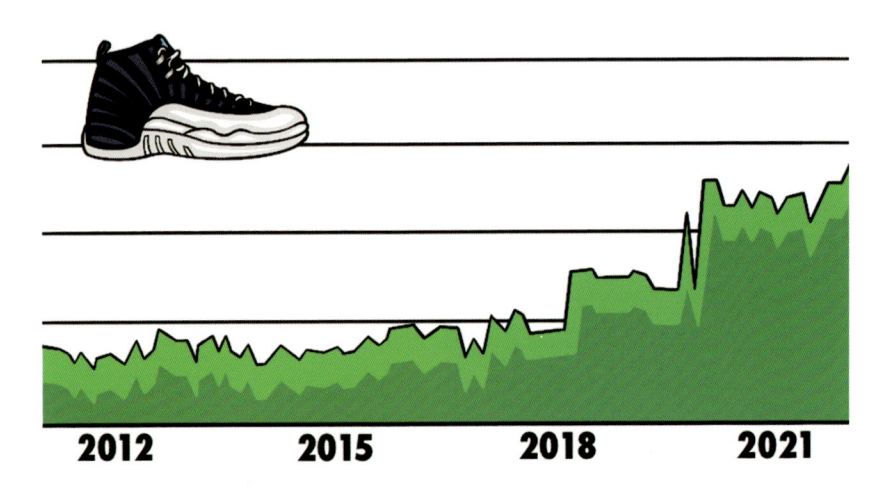

The 2016 Flu Games started out at around $250 and are now selling for $350.

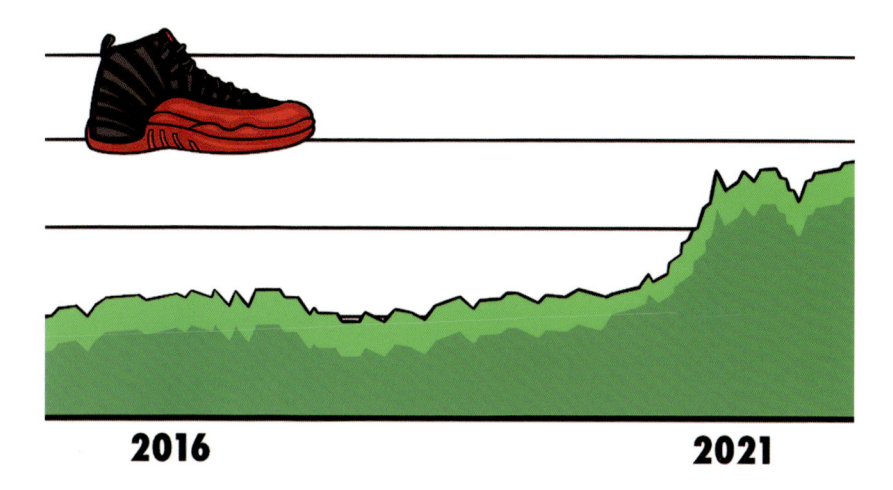

2012 Playoff 12s initially sold for $180 and are now selling for $360.

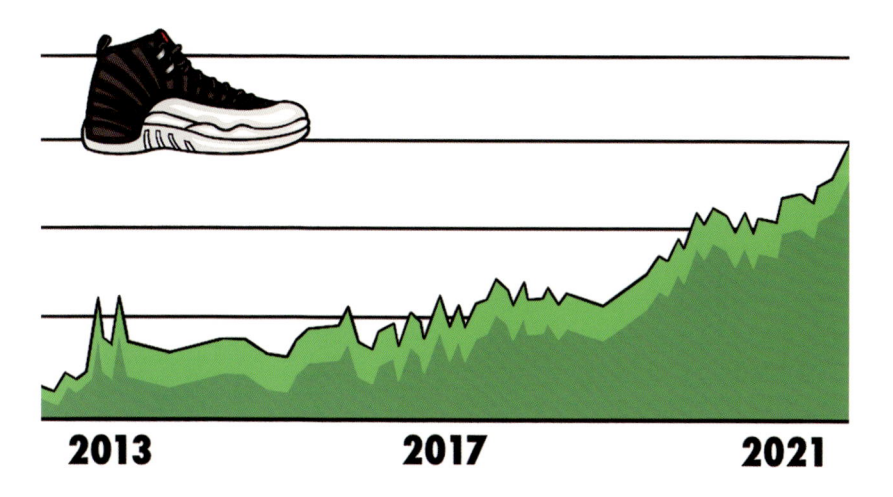

And finally, the 2016 French Blue 12s originally were being sold for $180 and are now at $350.

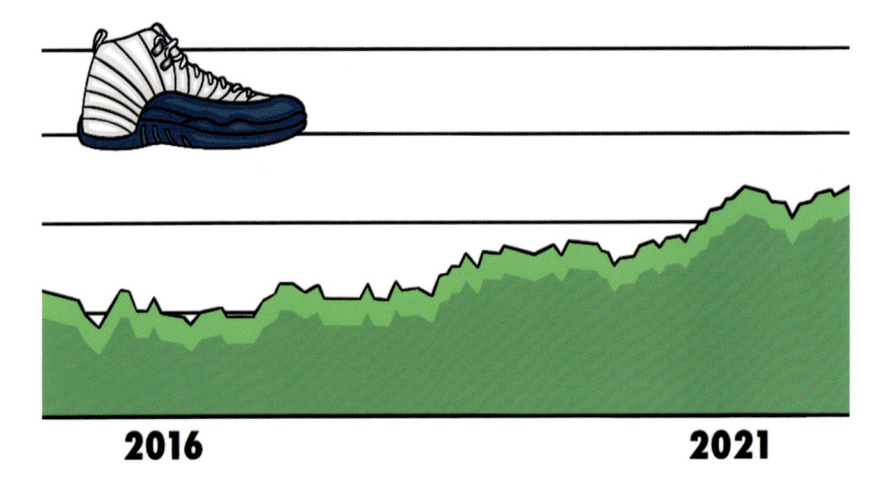

2016   **2021**

So, should we see future retros of these original colorways, expect prices to see a similar increase. However, Jordan 12's do take longer to go up, so you'll have to make a decision on whether you want to hold them for that long or if you would rather put your money into a different sneaker.

Jordan 13's

Jordan 13's has historically had a very low ceiling—meaning there is generally not enough room to hit the margins we are looking for. Also, Jordan 13's tend to take a long time to rise, so keep that in mind when investing. However, if understood properly, this model can be a safe investment. I do not recommend going too big into Jordan 13's, but it's not a bad idea to play with a couple pairs every once and awhile.

To start, there are three categories that I want to break up 13's into: Classic colorways, 13's with the Chicago color blocking, and miscellaneous colorways.

With classic colorways, we tend to see long-term trends similar to previous releases of the shoe. For example, the Jordan 13 "Bred" is one of the more iconic colorways of the 13. We saw a pair released in 2013, and then again in 2018. Looking at the prices of past releases, we could expect the 2018 pair to hit similar numbers to the 2013 pair. At the time of the 2018 release, the 2013 pair was selling for around $300, and the 2018 pair initially resold for around $190 as shown on the next page.

ART OF THE HOLD

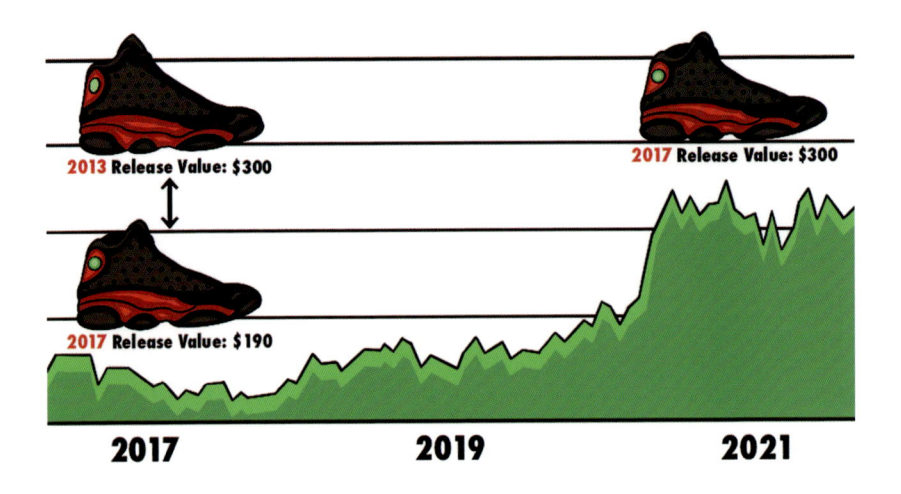

2013 Release Value: $300

2017 Release Value: $300

2017 Release Value: $190

2017   **2019**   **2021**

Thus, we could expect prices to rise to this same range over time—and as expected, prices rose from $190 to $310.

The Jordan 13 "He Got Game" is another classic Jordan 13 colorway that was released in 2013 and then again in 2018. At the time of the 2018 release, the 2013 pair was selling for around $380. Following that trend, prices on the 2018 pair started out at around $220 and have since gone to $370.

The Jordan 13 "Chicago" originally released in 1998 as one of the original colorways of the Jordan 13. And while this colorway can be looked at with the lens of an iconic colorway, I want to focus more on the color blocking. I've found that shoes with a similar color blocking perform like the Chicago 13's, so it's something you want to keep in mind when looking at potential Jordan 13 investments. When retroed in 2017, the Jordan 13 "Chicago" was initially selling for around $250. As usual with Jordan 13's, this shoe rose to around $300 in a relatively short amount of time (compared to most Jordan 13's). So, for future releases with similar color blocking, we could expect pairs to perform similarly. The Jordan 13 "Hyper Royal" used the same color-blocking as the Chicago 13's and initially was selling for around $200. So, we could anticipate prices rising to around $280-$300, following a similar trend to the Chicago's. As predicted, prices on the Hyper Royal 13's have reached $300. The Jordan 13 "Lakers" shares the same color-blocking as the Chicago and Hyper Royal 13's. Prices started out at $150, meaning there was room to make a strong margin. And again, as expected, prices of the Laker 13's have hit $280.

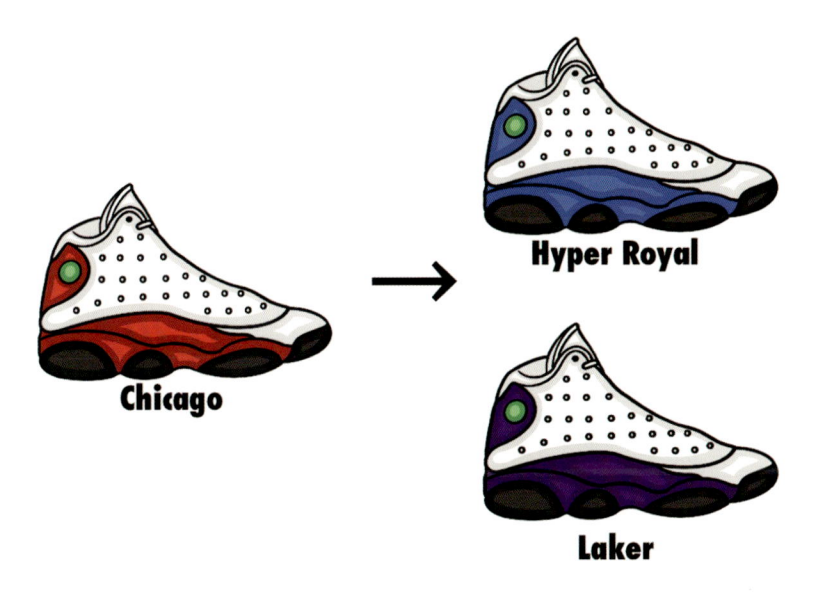

Chicago → **Hyper Royal**

Laker

For miscellaneous colorways, I tend to stay away, simply because the potential reward is usually not enough to warrant an investment. However, if you are looking to invest into a different Jordan 13 colorway, the strategies described earlier in this book will be helpful in identifying a strong hold.

Collaborations

When Nike collabs with another brand, we often see some of the most limited and most coveted releases. As a result, prices for said collabs can have incredible initial value and investment potential. In this chapter, we will break down some of the most notable collaborations in recent years and explain why they were a strong investment.

Off-White

Late 2017, Nike and Off-White released "The Ten," a series of reconstructed iconic Nike silhouettes. This marked the start of one of the most popular partnerships in sneakers from the last few years. At the time of this collection, Off-White was right at its peak in terms of mainstream visibility. It had just broken through as a top brand in both fashion and streetwear. Thus, when Off-White's creative element was applied to classic Nike sneakers, they were bound to be a hit. The price growth of this collection is as follows:

Which Shoes to Hold

Shoe Name	(Picture)	Original Price	Current Price
Off-White x Jordan 1 Chicago		$1500	$5000
Off-White x Nike Air Presto		$1000	$2400
Off-White x Nike React Hyperdunk		$420	$850
Off-White x Air Force 1 Low		$550	$2300
Off-White x Nike Blazer		$550	$1300
Off-White x Nike Air Max 90		$550	$1200
Off-White x Nike Air Max 97		$500	$1200
Off-White x Converse Chuck Taylor All-Star		$900	$1400
Off-White x Nike Zoom Fly		$450	$700
Off-White x VaporMax		$650	$1400

Again, prices started out at around $300 and jumped to over $1,000 a year after their release. For both pairs, the initial low buy-in cost paired with the extremely wearable colorways made these shoes highly in-demand, which eventually caused prices to rise.

TRAVIS SCOTT AF1 PATTERN

White Value: $300 → **White Value: $1000**

Sail Value: $300 → **Sail Value: $1000**

Later in 2018, we saw the release of the Cactus Jack 4: a wildly popular blue colorway on the iconic Jordan 4 silhouette. However, despite the popularity, initial prices started out as low as $320 due to the large number of pairs on the market. So, once pairs started to dry up, prices shot up—hitting over $1,000 in all sizes.

CACTUS JACK 4 SKYROCKET

2019 Value: $1000

2018 Value: $320

Seeing the early success of Travis Scott x Nike collaborations, it's easy to assume that all Travis Scott collabs will also go up in value. So, when the Jordan 6 Travis Scott released in 2019, many investors bought up pairs in hopes of seeing a similar return. But, this was not an Air Force 1 or a Jordan 4—it was a collab on the generally less-popular Jordan 6. Thus, this shoe was far less wearable than the previous collabs leading prices to plummet after the release day and remain stagnant ever since. Also in 2019, we saw a third Travis Scott Air Force 1 Low. However, in contrast to the previous Air Forces, this colorway was much harder to pull off. It's important to remember that wearability does not only refer to the silhouette, but the colorway too. So, seeing that less people would wear the shoe, prices on this Air Force 1 ended up dropping around $100 after release day and have not moved since. Other Travis Scott collaborations that had similar wearability issues include the Travis Scott Air Max 270 and the Travis Scott Jordan 33.

In certain cases, initial prices of a Travis Scott collab will start out high (sometimes too high). In these cases, we have to compare the values to similar sneakers. For example, both the Jordan 1 Travis Scott High and the Jordan 1 Travis Scott Low started out at around $1,000. So, we have to look at how other versions of these models have performed. We can compare the high-top version to other Jordan 1's like the Off-Whites and the Unions. Prices on these pairs range from $1,600–$6,000. So, assuming the same type of people would be buying the Travis Scott 1s, we can expect that people will be willing to pay more than $1,000 for the shoe—at minimum $1,600. As demand continued to build, we saw prices rise—hitting around $1,800 in all sizes.

Which Shoes to Hold

On the flip side, the Jordan 1 Travis Scott Low had no comparisons that were even close to $1,000 in value. As a result, we could understand that people may not be willing to pay more than a thousand dollars for this shoe. And as expected, prices have stayed around $1,000.

Another shoe that had a high initial resale value is the Travis Scott Nike SB Dunk low.

Prices on this pair started out at around $1,000 in all sizes. This model is different from the previously mentioned pairs because this was a part of the start of a Nike

SB Dunk "wave." Following the release of the Travis Scott Dunks, Nike released the Strangelove dunks as well as the Kentucky and Syracuse dunks. All of these pairs saw significant growth as the demand for dunks shot up again. As demand rose for dunks, so did the demand and thus prices for the Travis Scott pair.

Sacai and Ambush

Sacai is a popular Japanese luxury brand that was founded in 1999. When they partnered up with Nike to work on a line of sneakers, the shoes were met with high demand from Sacai supporters as well as sneakerheads. Due to the number of loyal supporters of Sacai as well as their now strong reputation within the sneaker community, there has always been a high level of visibility for Sacai sneakers. So, their investment value is determined mainly by their wearability and affordability.

First, let's look at the different models that Sacai has worked on. So far, we've seen a collab on a Nike Waffle, Blazer, and Vaporwaffle.

Each model tends to perform differently—for example, Sacai Blazers tend to stay in the $300–$400 range, giving them a generally low ceiling. With the other two silhouettes, prices depend more on the colorway. The design of the Sacai Waffle is already unique and is emphasized by the color blocking. Because Sacai is a fashion brand, consumers are more willing to take risks with their footwear (bright, unique designs) as opposed to the average Jordan sneakerhead. So, we are not limited to just the "safe" colorways.

The price growth of Sacai Waffles and Vaporwaffles can be seen on the next page.

Shoe Name	(Picture)	Original Price	Current Price
Sacai Waffle Blue Multi		$400	$700
Sacai Waffle Green Multi		$350	$650
Sacai Waffle Pine Green		$370	$500
Sacai Waffle Black		$570	$700
Sacai Waffle Summit White		$500	$700
Sacai Waffle Black Nylon		$280	$460
Sacai Waffle White Nylon		$200	$300
Sacai Vaporwaffle Black/White		$450	$470
Sacai Vaporwaffle Sport Fuschia		$400	$650
Sacai Vaporwaffle Tour Yellow		$400	$470
Sacai Vaporwaffle Villain Red		$420	$470

As shown, the Sacai collabs with the best margins were the ones that started out the lowest. Waffles that started out in the $200–$370 range saw the highest returns, proving the importance of considering affordability.

Another fashion brand who recently collabed with Nike that's worth mentioning is Ambush. Late in 2020, they released a black and white Dunk High—and while the shoe wasn't very popular with the sneakerhead community, it did extremely well with the fashion community, getting a lot of visibility with a lot of top models and influencers. As a result, prices jumped from $370-$650 in just two months. Even more recently, in February, Ambush released another Dunk, this time in an all-pink colorway. If this shoe gets the same attention in the fashion industry as the black/white pair did, then we could see a similar increase in price.

Other Sneaker Stores

Occasionally, Nike chooses to work with an actual sneaker store on a collaboration—most notably Concepts, Trophy Room, and Atmos. These collaborations generally give the designers a lot of room to build a story and get creative. These stories behind the shoes build visibility as well as cultivate desirability and thus demand.

Concepts created the idea of the Lobster Dunks as a way to represent the city of Boston.

ART OF THE HOLD

They went all out with their campaign, creating rumors in the media, new sneaker technology, packaging, release types, and sneaker design overall.

LOBSTER DUNK CONCEPT

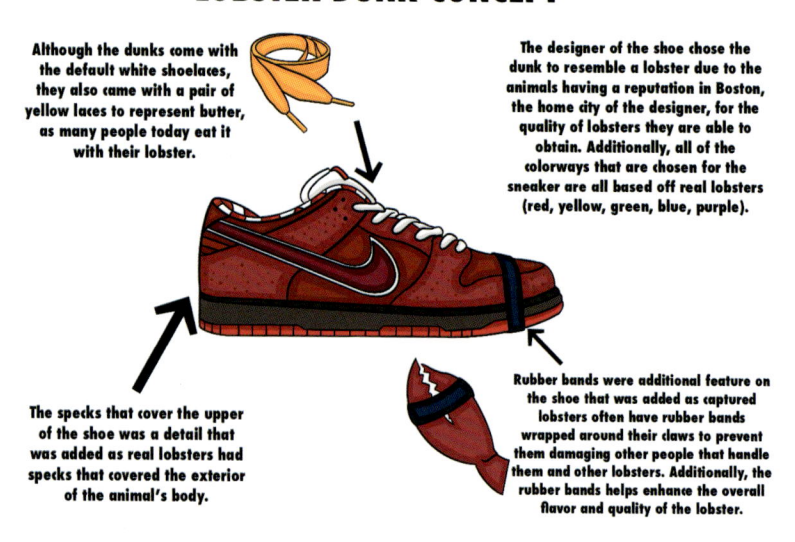

Although the dunks come with the default white shoelaces, they also came with a pair of yellow laces to represent butter, as many people today eat it with their lobster.

The designer of the shoe chose the dunk to resemble a lobster due to the animals having a reputation in Boston, the home city of the designer, for the quality of lobsters they are able to obtain. Additionally, all of the colorways that are chosen for the sneaker are all based off real lobsters (red, yellow, green, blue, purple).

The specks that cover the upper of the shoe was a detail that was added as real lobsters had specks that covered the exterior of the animal's body.

Rubber bands were additional feature on the shoe that was added as captured lobsters often have rubber bands wrapped around their claws to prevent them damaging other people that handle them and other lobsters. Additionally, the rubber bands helps enhance the overall flavor and quality of the lobster.

As the story of the Lobster Dunks continued to grow, so did the hype. Every sneakerhead was excited to see what Concepts would do next, and everyone was following the story. Even after the campaign was over, people were drawn to the sneakers, causing prices of all Lobster Dunks to reach over $1,000.

Trophy Room is owned by Michael Jordan's son, so they have access to a lot more resources than most when

Which Shoes to Hold

it comes to collaborations. Jordan's son Marcus places a heavy emphasis on capturing a moment or feeling from his father's career through sneakers. Recently, we saw the release of the Jordan 1 "Trophy Rooms" which commemorated the infamous "freeze out" in the 1985 All-Star game. Largely as a result of this commemoration, prices on this shoe are sitting at over $2,500.

Atmos is a USA/Japan founded in 2000 by Hommyo Hidefumi. They began by focusing on selling vintage Nike sneakers—buying pairs in the US and bringing them to Japan and vice versa. Naturally, this meant that Atmos was selling a lot of Nike Air Maxes so their brand quickly became tied to the shoe. Thus, when Nike was deciding who to work with for the 2017 Air Max Day, Atmos was the obvious choice. As a company that was started based on the Air Max, Atmos had a strong understanding of who was buying Air Maxes and what type of shoe they would want. They created the Nike Air Max 1 Atmos Elephant, which quickly became an iconic sneaker.

Like with most iconic pairs, the demand is steady, even almost three years after the release. So as pairs on the market started to dry up, prices have risen from $350 to $1,000.

Application

As evidenced by the examples given in this section, we can recognize that collaborations play a major role in the sneaker market. There are a few key takeaways that you can use to analyze future collaborations. First, make sure that the silhouette and colorway have demand. A collab on an unpopular sneaker will not perform well. Second, compare initial prices to similar models—if the initial value is above what most other pairs are selling for, they may be overpriced, regardless of demand. Third, it's important to look at the consumer base of the brand/company that is working on the sneaker. The collaboration may not be targeted towards sneakerheads, so you must consider other markets and communities. Finally, make sure you understand the power of storytelling in regard to sneaker releases. A story can play a huge role in building hype and demand for a sneaker, so it should not be overlooked.

Outlet Holds

Certain shoes end up in outlets and reach such discounted prices that they simply cannot go down any lower. For these sneakers, it's typically a relatively low buy-in cost and an overall safe investment. Given, not every sneaker that ends up at the outlets will rise in value—you must still take into account the wearability and visibility as well as compare the shoe with similar models and colorways. An example of a good outlet investment is the Jordan 4 "Pure Money." Released in 2017, this shoe not only sat on shelves, but was discounted all the way down to $110 at one point. So, clearly this shoe is affordable. They've got one of the most if not the most wearable colorways—triple white. And the 2006 version of the same shoe was hovering at $300–$400 in all sizes. That same shoe that was on sale for $110 is now at $400 to $500 depending on the size, which would mean a 400%-500% return (in 2–3 years) on a shoe that couldn't even originally sell out. An extremely similar recent example, the Jordan 4 "Winterized Loyal Blue" also fell to $110 in all sizes. In around 8 months, the shoe doubled in value, and is now selling for around $280 in all sizes. We also have to mention the Jordan 1 "Phantom Gym Red" GS, and the Jordan 1 "Bloodline" GS.

Both of these shoes sat at their retail price of $120 for months (even popping up at my outlets for $69.99 at one point) before showing some growth and eventually taking off. I think that these examples highlight the incredible demand for grade school Jordan 1's as a whole. While the Phantom Gym Red is a more unique and wearable shoe, the Bloodline's aren't necessarily anything special. However, we cannot ignore the iconic use of a black and red colorway on a Jordan 1. The female audience places less value on the "classic" color-blocking, as opposed to the male sneakerheads who generally were not a fan of this shoe. This is clearly shown as the grade school prices are more than $100 above the men's, despite the men's pairs having a higher retail price.

Used Shoes

Essentially, as the price of a deadstock shoe goes up, the price of a used shoe goes up. Thus, you can lower your buy-in cost by buying used shoes and see similar margins. However, you won't be able to acquire bulk of used shoes, so this is only something you should do when starting out or when you're working with low capital. If you're ever tempted to buy a pair for personal wear, you can buy a used pair of shoes that you think will go up, and your "personal pair" can end up turning into a profitable investment for you.

Which sizes to buy

The sizes you choose to buy depend entirely on the group of people who will be buying the shoes. For example, if you think a shoe will be most popular with girls, you'll want to focus on grade school sizes (5.5y–7y). If you think a shoe will be a hit in Asia/newer Jordan 1 hypebeasts, you'll want to focus on the smaller men's sizes (7.5–9.5). If you think a shoe will do the best with the OG sneakerhead crowd/newer hypebeasts, focus on larger men's sizes (10-13). For example, with Jordan 1 "CO Japan Neutral Grey," most people who will be wearing the shoe are girls. The silver and shiny colorway just doesn't cater to what's popular or deemed acceptable for the average man's footwear. Thus, if you plan on investing in this shoe, you should only buy grade school sizes. This is exemplified by the current market values of this shoe in different sizes. Sales for men's pairs average a mere 35% over retail price while sales for grade school pairs average a staggering 95% over retail price. A shoe that you would want to buy smaller men's sizes would be a hyped-up release like the Jordan 1 "Travis Scott." An example of a shoe where you would want to target larger sizes would be a classic colorway of a less-mainstream model such as the Jordan 6 "Infrared." For this shoe, sizes 11.5+ are going for around $80 more than sizes 11 and below. This often holds true for other models such as the Jordan 11, Jordan 13, and the Jordan 5.

For reference, below is a chart of how certain sizes perform in the current Jordan 1 market.

Which Shoes to Hold

JORDAN 1 SIZING GUIDE

- **3.5y-** Priced highest on release date, does poorly long term- hard to find buyers

- **4y-4.5y-** Perform well for Jordan 1 Mid's and Low's, but not as well for Jordan 1 High

- **5y-5.5y-** Prime size range

- **6y-6.5y-** Used to be the most profitable sizes on release but Nike has begun producing more pairs to meet the demand, regardless does very well long-term.

- **7y-** Most common size, typically priced lowest on release date but highest long term.

- **7.5-** Prices are usually volatile as not many pairs are produced in this size. This size is often the most valuable due to its rarity.

- **8-9-** Easy to buy/easy to sell. They used to go for the most (after size 7.5), but the gap between these sizes and other mens sizes has started to shrink.

- **9.5-10-** Very easy to buy and easy to sell- slightly less value than sizes 8-9 but slightly more value than sizes 10.5+.

- **10.5, 11, 12, 13-** Highly produced sizes, typically on the lower end of value. Certain Jordan 1's are more expensive in these sizes (like SBB 3.0)- bigger sizes are starting to jump more.

- **11.5, 12.5-** Rarer sizes to find which leads to a small jump in value when compared to other sizes 10.5+. Size 11.5 is very easy to sell, and you can price them higher than similar sizes.

CHAPTER 5

WHICH SHOES NOT TO HOLD

For every one sneaker that is a good investment, there are ten more that are bad investments. This chapter looks at a couple of major examples where many people thought a shoe would be a good investment, but it wasn't. Identifying a bad investment is equally as important as picking a good investment. Taking the time to understand why a shoe won't go up can help tremendously.

In order for a sneaker to go up in value, regular people have to be buying them, not just resellers. Oftentimes resellers will all start buying up a certain shoe, driving prices up, but when they realize there is not much demand yet, the market quickly crashes. The number of pairs supplied at that high "bubble" price greatly outweighs the number of pairs demanded, which leads to a short-term surplus of pairs on the market before sellers start to undercut. A classic example of this is the Jordan 1 Satin Black Toe; in the weeks after their release, prices shot up to

ART OF THE HOLD

around $1,000 in most sizes. The majority of resellers had been buying up pairs as they thought they would rise even higher in value. However, they failed to understand that the average customer who would be buying these shoes would not be willing to spend $1,000+. And in reality, regular people were not buying at that price. This proved to be an expensive lesson for many as prices dropped all the way down to $400. Many resellers refer to this failed investment as their biggest mistake—all because they believed in a bubble. A more recent example of a bubble is the Jordan 1 Low "Reverse Bred" GS.

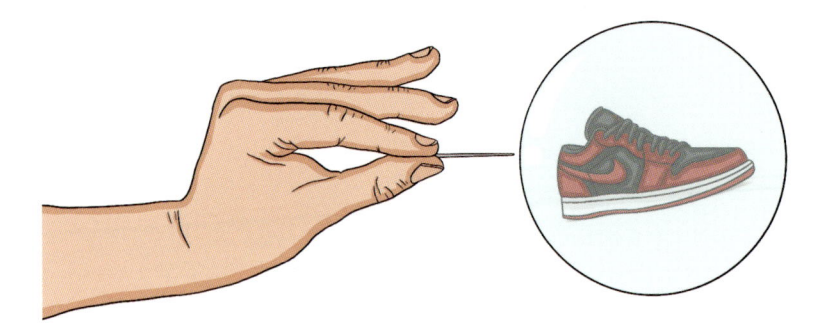

Again, almost every reseller started buying up pairs as they were confident they would rise in value. The shoe hit $125 in all sizes, and one month later, is now sitting at $85 per size (retail is $80). Many resellers are stuck with hundreds of pairs because they got caught up in a bubble as well as the fear of missing out. The reality is, the number of pairs on the market is overwhelmingly higher than the number of actual buyers. This is an example of there being too many pairs of a shoe. The only way a shoe will rise in value is if the number of pairs demanded at a price outweighs the number of pairs supplied at that price. If the number of pairs demanded can never reach the number of pairs supplied, the shoe will never go up in value.

However, you cannot simply rely on the stock numbers to tell you if there are "too many" pairs on the market. The stock numbers must be compared to the demand—a highly produced shoe still can go up if there is enough demand. An extremely limited sneaker can also go down if there is not enough demand. For example, the Jordan 10 "Solefly" was released in very low quantities, and, because of the exclusivity and the nature of the collaboration, many people expected the shoe to rise in value.

However, there was almost no demand for the shoe, leading to prices settling at around $245 in all sizes. The reason behind this is that the shoe is simply not wearable enough to justify a high price. Almost every Jordan 10 (along with Jordan 2's, Jordan 8's, Jordan 9's, and Jordan 10's) will not be a strong investment due to the lack of demand. This leads me to my third point—the shoe has to be wearable enough to the point where the masses will want to buy them. I made a controversial video a while back, saying that the Jordan 6 "Travis Scott" would go down in value. If you go back to my video, 99% of the comments disagreed, explaining how the Jordan 6 was, in fact, wearable, and because it was a Travis Scott collaboration, they will go up. At the time of the video, prices were at $1,000 in all sizes. Now, they sit at $650.

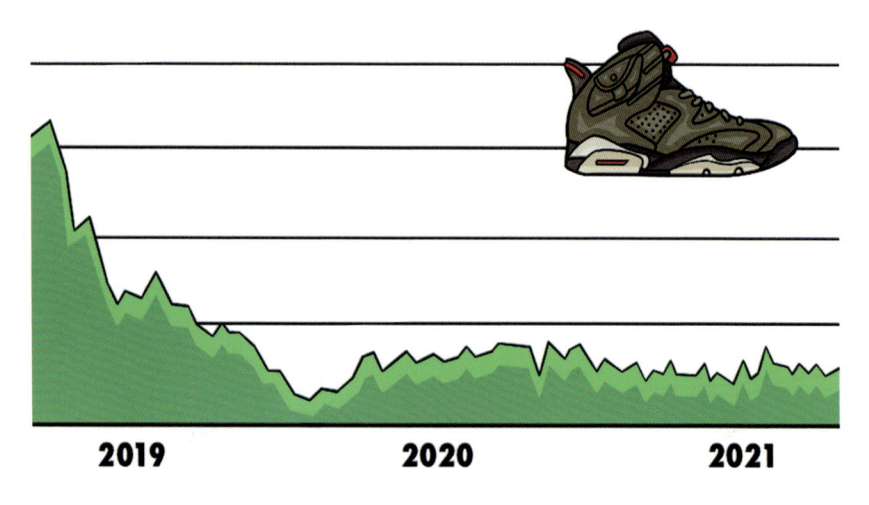

2019　　　　　　**2020**　　　　　　**2021**

In my most controversial video, I detailed why the Chunky Dunky SB would not go up in value. While the concept sounded good, the shoe itself simply is not wearable. Further, prices started out extremely high compared to similar models, meaning that this shoe failed to meet both our wearability and affordability checks. In summary, you should avoid investing into shoes that too many other resellers are buying-in to, shoes that start out too high, and shoes that are simply unwearable for the general public because of their undesirable silhouette or colorway.

Margins

It's also important to consider your buy-in cost in relation to your expected profit. A shoe with a lower buy-in cost will almost always yield higher margins than a more expensive shoe. For example, if you were to invest into a Jordan 1 Low at $100 a pair, you would hit a 50% return when the shoe hits $150. However, if you were to invest into a sneaker at $400 a pair, they would need to hit $600 to reach that same 50% margin. So, it's key that you don't get caught up in the hype and always invest into the most hyped, expensive pairs—you can often make more profit with less hyped, cheaper shoes.

Women's shoes

One of the easiest mistakes to make when starting out is analyzing a women's shoe the same way you would look at a men's shoe. And while some male sneakerheads don't have a problem wearing a women's shoe, most male consumers will stay away. Thus, even when a colorway is strong and prices start out low in comparison to a men's pair, it's not always a sound investment. I'd like to bring up a couple examples where many investors made this mistake. The first is the Jordan 1 "Satin Black Toe." Beyond the fact that the initial prices were too high, the fact that it was a women's shoe helped lead to the crash in value. At the time of the release, the men's version of the shoe (released in 2016) was selling for around $800. Thus, it was reasonable to assume that a re-release would perform similarly—but this wasn't simply a re-release, this was a women's version. Thus, prices for the women's pair could not sustainably remain higher than the men's pair, and they were bound to drop in value. Another example of a shoe that many people treated as a men's pair is the Jordan 1 "Satin Snakeskin." With a colorway similar to the coveted Jordan 1 "Chicago," many people assumed this would be a very profitable investment.

And if they were a men's pair, there's a good chance that they would have been. However, the fact that they were a women's release meant that the investment potential of the shoe decreased substantially. I made a controversial video when they released predicting that they would go down in value (which they did) because I was able to understand the impact that being a women's release can have on a shoe's value. However, there still is some potential for pairs that start low enough. But even if a shoe might go up, the market for women's pairs is volatile enough to where I wouldn't recommend going near it unless you really had a strong understanding of the trends. Specific examples of women's shoes that were strong investments are the Jordan 1 Blue Chill, Jordan 1 Lucky Green, and Jordan 4 Fossil. For these pairs, bigger sizes tend to perform better seeing as men will often wear these types of women's shoes.

Jordan 2

By far the least popular silhouette of Jordan's 1–14, this shoe has such low demand that Nike has only released one Jordan 2 in each of the past three years—the most recent of which can be found for a mere $100. In this section, we'll explain why you should stay away from investing into Jordan 2s if Nike releases more pairs in the future.

Nike designed the Jordan 2 with the intent of creating a more premium, sophisticated basketball sneaker in comparison to the well-received Jordan 1. They even bumped up the retail price of the Jordan 2 to a staggering $100—as opposed to the $65 retail price of the Jordan 1. Jordan debuted the sneaker on the court during the 1986–87 season, wearing both mid and low top versions of the silhouette. Since then, Nike has released a few Jordan 2 colorways and collaborations worth looking into, most notably the Jordan 2 Eminem and the Jordan 2 Just Don pack.

I want to bring up the Eminem 2s to compare their prices with the Eminem 4s. These two shoes are comparable in terms of both the collaboration and the exclusivity. However, the silhouette sets them apart. The Jordan 4 Eminem has sold for around $20,000 while the Jordan 2 Eminem sells for around $3,500. The other most talked about Jordan 2 collaboration is with Just Don. Nike released a blue colorway in 2015 with a retail price of $350. The collaboration had a lot of hype behind it, leading to resale prices starting out upwards of $1,300. However, that hype eventually died down, and the prevailing lack of demand dropped prices all the way down to around $600. Following a similar trend, Nike and Just Don teamed up again in 2016 to release a more premium beach colorway that retailed at $650. Again, seeing a wave of hype leading up the release, initial prices started out at around $1200. This shoe has since fallen all the way down to around $400, $250 under retail price. So, we can clearly see that even a Jordan 2 with as much hype as the Just Don pairs had cannot sustain a high price.

Jordan 5

Before getting into why Jordan 5's are generally not a strong investment, I want to acknowledge the potential of strong outlet Jordan 5 investments. You can see solid margins on a Jordan 5 that starts out around $100–$180. However, the problem with most Jordan 5's is that they have an extremely low ceiling. The vast majority of Jordan 5's will not reach anywhere above $300, most not even hitting $250. And even if they do hit $250, it often takes upwards of a year to do so, making the investment almost always not worth it.

The past two years, we've seen a handful of Jordan 5 releases, almost all performing similarly. The Jordan 5 Fire Red, Alternate Bel-Air, Michigan, Top 3, Oregon, and Alternate Grape all saw initial resale prices of around $200. And each of these shoes remain under $220 today.

release. From there, prices have gradually risen back up to around $290. Both the 2014 White Infrared 6's and the 2015 Maroon 6's steadily decreased for a couple years after the release before steadily increasing starting in 2019. The more recent 2019 Black Infrared 6's have seen steady growth but have taken around two years for the margins to be worth an investment. With all these pairs, there is generally a ceiling of around $350–$400. So, we can see that even in the original colorways, the margins are too low to justify holding pairs for so long.

This lack of investment potential is highlighted by the Jordan 6 Travis Scott. Following its release in 2019, many people assumed it would be a strong investment because of the nature of the collaboration. However, after prices started out over $1,100, it was clear that this shoe would go nowhere but down. The Jordan 6 silhouette in general does not have enough demand to sustain these prices, so naturally, the sneaker dropped down to $550—half of what they were selling for on release day.

In summary, while some Jordan 6's do rise in value, they take years to do so. In addition, there is generally a ceiling of around $350–$400, lowering the investment potential even further. As a result, I advise staying away from investing into Jordan 6's and focusing on some of the more profitable models.

Jordan 7

Jordan 7's are almost never strong investments, with the exception of outlet pairs. If we look back at some of the past releases, we can see that most Jordan 7's actually went down in value. However, prices all spiked up at the same time as a result of the Last Dance documentary. This documentary is not something that will happen again, so it's best to look at the charts without this spike in order to get a sense of how pairs have performed and how pairs will perform in the future.

There were five original Jordan 7 colorways released in 1992: the Jordan 7 Bordeaux, Olympic, Raptors, Cardinals, and Hares.

Each of these colorways have been rereleased in the past 10 years, and each pair have performed similarly. Prices often start out high before slowly dipping down to around $200–$240. From there, prices tend to plateau until the eventual Last Dance spike. So, we can expect future releases of these original colorways to perform similarly—starting out high then dropping down to around $200–$240.

The only Jordan 7's really worth investing into are outlet pairs that start out at around $90–$110 per pair. This gives you enough room to make a strong margin despite the lack of real demand for Jordan 7's. Two of the most notable examples of Jordan 7 outlet holds are the Jordan 7 Pantone and Jordan 7 Pure Platinum. Each of these pairs released in 2017 and quickly hit the outlets. At the time, you could find pairs for around $100. Since then, prices on both pairs have jumped to around $250, which would have given you a 150% return. Look out for future Jordan 7's to hit the outlets and try to buy-in at that target price of around $100.

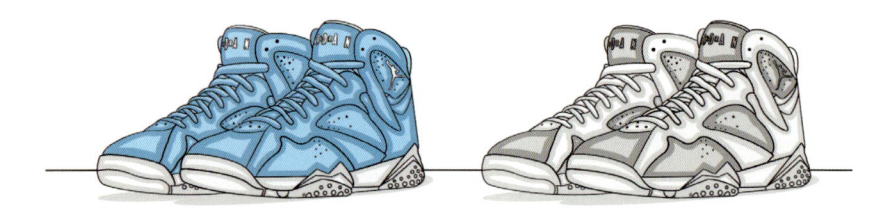

Jordan 8

Almost all Jordan 8s are not strong investments simply due to their lack of wearability. The multiple straps and overall design give the shoe a messier look to some of the more well-liked Jordan silhouettes.

On top of that, the Jordan 8 is one of the heavier models and is generally one of the least breathable. So, there is not much incentive for people to purchase a pair for themselves. In fact, Nike lost so much confidence in the model that they didn't release any men's pairs of the Jordan 8 in all of 2020. If Nike doesn't think that they can sell pairs, there's no reason for us to think otherwise.

The only two real exceptions to this are the Jordan 8 OVO's and the Jordan 8 Aqua—both of which still only see less than a 50% increase in multiple years. The Jordan 8

Aqua is by far the most recognized colorway for the silhouette, and still can't break past $350. The OVO 8's saw a little bit of hype because of the collaboration but still ended up selling for near retail for nearly two years following the release.

So, for future Jordan 8 releases it is best not to invest into pairs as you will likely see no significant return due to the overall lack of demand.

Jordan 9

The Jordan 9 released in 1993 and was the first Jordan silhouette to come out after Michael Jordan first retired from basketball. The model in general never really gained too much hype, especially with the newer sneakerheads. As a result, even if some pairs do go up, Jordan 9's are generally a tougher shoe to sell. Just for comparison, both the Jordan 9 Pearl Blue and Jordan 1 Turbo Green released in February of 2019. In the past 12 months, there have been 3,700 Turbo Green sales on Stock X while only 600 Pearl Blue sales. This can offer some type of insight into the contrast in demand.

Similarly, to the Jordan 6, many Jordan 9's will see a dip in price before eventually returning to their original value. For example, the 2015 Jordan 9 Anthracite was initially selling for around $220 before dropping down to $150 and then going all the way back up to $250. The 2014 Jordan 9 Barons started out at $275, dropped down to $160, then went back up to $275. For each of these examples, the cycle took almost five years to complete—so it's clear that they weren't worth investing into, even if you buy the dip.

Some pairs do see steady growth, but again, it takes years for the margins to be worth the investment. A few examples of stronger Jordan 9 holds include the Jordan 9 Pearl Blue, Racer Blue, and City of Flight. Each of these pairs was initially selling for around $150 and have since gone up to $250.

However, it took around two years for this growth to happen. So, while you may find value in stashing a couple pairs away and forgetting about them for a couple years, it's not usually the best use of your capital and really isn't a scalable investment as you would have trouble selling pairs in high quantities years after the release.

Jordan 10

The Jordan 10 can most closely be compared to the Jordan 9 in terms of resale and investment potential. There is not much demand for the silhouette in general, so even the rare pair that does go up a little is usually not worth investing into. In fact, the Jordan 10 has even less demand than the Jordan 9—partially because most of the pairs that Jordan Brand released look almost identical to each other.

Almost every year since 2012, Jordan Brand has dropped a Jordan 10 with the same color blocking as the original 1994 Jordan 10 Steel colorway. In 2012, we got the Jordan 10 Chicago Bulls, in 2010—the Steel 10's, in 2014—the Powder Blue 10's, in 2015—the Double Nickel 10's, in 2018—the Orlando 10's, and in 2019—the Seattle 10's.

If you compare each of these colorways, you'll see they all look pretty much identical, with only a couple changes in color. This makes it almost impossible for pairs to rise in value as buyers are likely to always just buy whichever pair they can find for the cheapest—they all act as substitute goods for each other and as a result, all keep each other's value down.

Similarly, to the Jordan 8's, the Jordan 10's also got a collaboration with OVO (Drake's brand). Like the 8's, there was almost no visible OVO branding on the shoe, so despite the initial hype because of the collaboration, demand and value quickly dropped off. Both the white and the black pair started out selling for around $600 and $500 respectively and are now selling for only $300.

If an OVO collaboration could not create consistent demand for a pair, then we can expect little demand for a regular Jordan 10.

CHAPTER 6

WHEN TO BUY-IN

In this chapter, we explain the different times you may want to buy-in, depending on your capital, time, and patience. As we dive further into the chapter, we will also cover what I like to call *"the art of the dip."*

It is important to have a buy-in price in mind before you start looking for pairs, and sometimes even before a release. Although sometimes you have to be flexible regarding your buy-in prices, I typically recommend sticking to your number. You can generally find this number through comparisons with similar models as well as understanding how high you expect the shoe to rise. I generally try to underpredict what I think a shoe will hit to limit any risk. As an example, we will look at the Yeezy 350 V2 "Bred." Even before the release, we knew that this sneaker would eventually rise in value; however, we needed the prices to hit a certain mark for the margins to be worth the investment. We looked at the market of the earlier release, as well as stock numbers, and recognized that to achieve the margins we wanted, we needed to buy-in at around $330–$360 per pair. If they didn't reach that range, and stayed around $450, we would not invest into them. At the time that I am writing this, bae sizes are going for around $450 and bigger sizes are going for around $430. Again, if this shoe didn't drop to our target range, we would have passed on them. Even if a sneaker goes up, if the price starts out too high, the margins may not be ideal.

Once you have your buy-in price, you have to figure out when the shoe will hit that price and how long they will stay at that price. If a shoe doesn't start to go up until after 4 months, it's better to buy your pairs at the end of those 4 months in order to make the most out of your time and money.

The typical flow for Jordan 1's right now is somewhat confusing at first glance but makes sense when you break it down. First, the pre-release price depends solely on visibility and how many early pairs are available. If a shoe goes relatively unnoticed up until its release (think Jordan 1 Midnight Navy), then the early prices will be low. However, if the hype is there pre-release (think Jordan 1 Mocha), then the early prices will be high. These early prices tend to go down leading up to the release as the appeal for having an early pair goes down. Why pay $300 for a shoe when you have a chance of getting it for $170 in a couple of days. However, right after the release, assuming the sneaker was limited enough, we see a rise in prices as people start to take their L's online. They were hoping to secure their pair on release day for retail, and when they can't, they go straight to the aftermarket to secure their pairs. This carries on through the day until there's a slight drop in the number of people buying pairs every hour. As resellers start to get pairs in from online orders, prices again start to drop as the undercutting begins. People who need the money quickly are happy with any amount of profit, and seeing prices start to drop, most sellers want to move their pairs as soon as possible.

There's an important distinction between "resellers" and "investors." The resellers are the ones who either paid retail or paid low enough to where they can make a quick profit. The investors are the ones who are trying to time the market in an attempt to make a solid investment. Because the majority of "investors" don't fully understand the market, many believe that the best time to buy-in is always right after online pairs come in. As these "investors" start to buy up pairs, prices start to rise, causing others to start buying pairs themselves so they don't miss out on the opportunity. However, this first rise in price is generally a bubble, and once people realize that they can't move pairs for that high price yet, prices fall back down. A great example of this happening is with the Jordan 1 "Royal." Many investors, including myself, started buying-in on pairs causing prices to initially be inflated. However, after a short period of time, the inflated prices quickly dropped back down before eventually plateauing for a few months. It's oftentimes smart to buy pairs before this "bubble" and sell them at the top of the run, right before the bubble pops. However, this is only possible if you separate yourself from the general FOMO (fear of missing out) that sometimes dictates the short-term market. Trust in your research and trust in your intuition. Once prices fall back down after the bubble, there is usually a time where prices don't move much as the market settles. This period could be for 2 months, 6 months, or even a year—all depending on visibility and stock numbers. For newer investors who are looking to make long-term investments, this period where the market has settled is often the ideal time to buy-in. Generally, you can wait around a month or two to really gauge how the sneaker is being received by the public. If you notice a sense of hype building around them, or see a wave of influencers start to promote them, then that might be a good time to buy-in. For example, if you see people on TikTok (think Charli D'Amelio) wearing them, then you might want to buy-in sooner rather than later. If you don't hear much about the shoes at all or don't see much change in demand, then you can continue waiting.

Art of the Dip

As important as it is to recognize which shoes will eventually rise in value, it's also important to identify pairs that will see a dip before they take off. This dip is the ideal time for you to buy-in. Generally, a dip will occur when the demand for a shoe has been overestimated or the stock numbers are too high to sustain a high resale price. For example, the Jordan 1 "Black Gym Red" saw initial resale prices of $270. They then jumped up to $300 and most investors hoped they'd keep rising. However, resellers quickly realized that there was not enough demand to move pairs at $300, and as a result, they started undercutting to quickly sell off their pairs. The value ended up tanking to the point where pairs were selling for around $200. I was able to identify this dip and made the call for my chat to buy-in at an average of $200–$220 per pair. While I knew that they would go up from this dip, I also understood that I would need to wait 4–5 months for the demand to go back up.

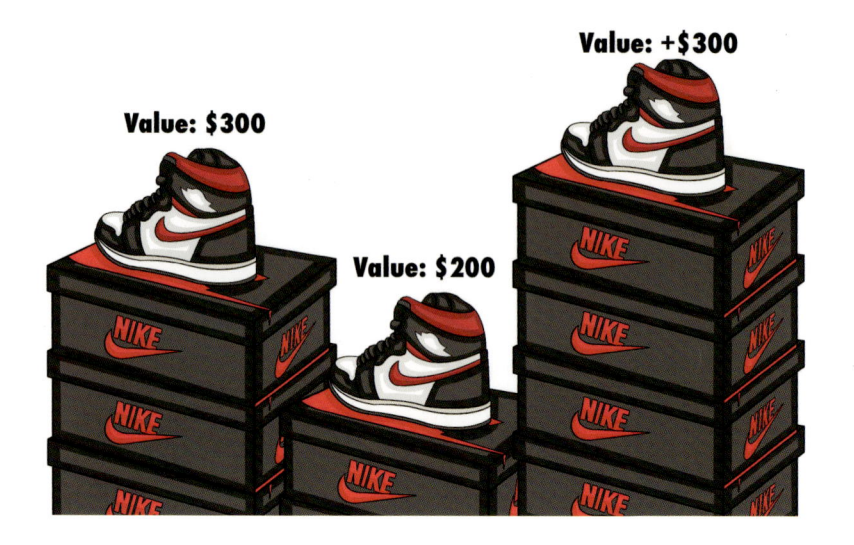

Since then, they've gone back up to around $300 per pair meaning you would be profiting an average of $100 per pair.

Another example of a shoe that saw a dip is the Jordan 13 "Flint." In this case, the initial demand was very high, but the stock numbers were even higher. After the release, pairs were selling extremely quickly for upwards of $300. I made a video after the release predicting the dip—now, at the time that I'm writing this book, pairs are selling for around $220. If the Jordan 13 "Flint" was a shoe that you wanted to invest in, now could be the time to do so.

CHAPTER 7

BULK BUYING

I get messages every day from people who are asking where I buy my shoes. Oftentimes they see the hundreds of pairs I post on social media and assume all those pairs come from one person. While some of the more recent buyouts did come from one seller, I started out buying from 20+ different sellers in order to secure the quantities that I wanted. Overall, where you buy depends a lot on how many pairs you are looking to purchase as well as how much time you are willing to spend buying. It may be reasonable for you to buy from individual sellers if you are only looking to buy 20 pairs of a shoe, but if you're looking for high quantities, it'll be much easier to buy in bulk from a single seller. In this chapter, I'll cover specifically how I handle each of these ways of buying shoes.

Generally speaking, the key is to get as many people to see that you're buying, and for you to see as many people as possible who are selling. To begin, you can build a following on your social media accounts—but it's also possible

ART OF THE HOLD

to do this without any following. For Facebook, most sellers will have individual pairs that were purchased in-store. After joining all your local sneaker groups, make a WTB (want to buy) post in the following format:

Jordan 1 Mocha's used for example

BANNED LA
GROUP POST BY SNEAKER INVEST
JUST NOW

WTB ALL MOCHA I'S
BUYING ALL JORDAN I MOCHAS
ANY QUANTITY, ANY SIZE – BUYING ALL
CASH READY

RANDOM BUMP GETS $50

LIKE   COMMENT   SHARE

This format is extremely effective as the incentivized "bumping" will bring your post to the top of the group. From this, you will maximize your visibility to potential sellers. Even if you are only buying a certain number of pairs, this post format will bring you the most options, which will allow you to pick the best priced deals.

For Instagram, you can follow a similar approach, using resources created specifically for resellers to gain visibility. There are certain accounts who get 20,000 story views that will repost your WTB stories if you tag them. The format for these posts should look something like this:

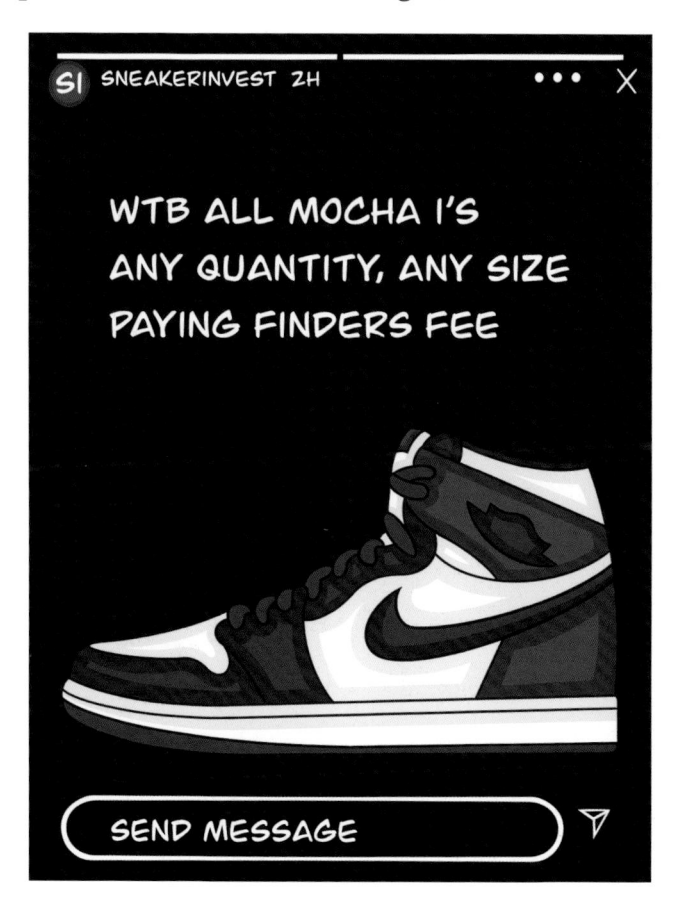

You can use a similar concept for Twitter, where sellers generally have bulk pairs that they purchased through botting. Once you've built up a decent following (through engaging with other accounts in the community), make a post saying:

> **SNEAKER INVEST**
> @SNEAKERINVEST
>
> BUYING ALL MOCHA 1'S
> ANY QUANTITY ANY SIZE
> RANDOM RT GETS $100 ONCE PAIRS ARE FOUND
>
> 2:06 PM · 2/06/21 TWITTER FOR IPHONE
>
> VIEW TWEET ACTIVITY
>
> 154 RETWEETS 234 LIKES

On the flip side, in order to see as many sellers as possible, you can use these same resources. On Facebook, scroll through your local sneaker groups, offering on any pairs you are interested in. On Instagram, you can use those same accounts that repost stories, and look through the reposted stories yourself. You can also build up a list of sellers who you follow and know are legit. Eventually, if you continue to spend money with the same people, they will reward your loyalty with "first dibs" on any bulk or even sometimes discounted prices. It is essential that you build and maintain relationships with your sellers.

Beyond social media platforms, you can also take advantage of a plethora of marketplaces. These can include, but are not limited to, eBay, OfferUp, Mercari, Poshmark, Grailed, Stockx, and Goat. Typically, prices are higher on these sites due to the selling fees (except eBay), but sometimes you will find a good deal.

As a last recommendation, I generally advise not telling people or broadcasting that you are buying a shoe with intentions of holding them. As you start to build a reputation with successful investments, sellers may start to feel like they should just hold their pairs themselves and not sell to you. Something you can do to avoid this is to say you are buying for a store, and that "pairs are just selling faster than we can keep them on the shelves." This eliminates any hesitation a seller might have in selling their pairs.

Deal Breakdown

1. After finding a bulk seller who has a sneaker you're looking to buy, you reach out to him: "Hey—saw you had bulk of _____—what are sizes and pricing for all? Payment ready."

2. You then wait for his response:
   a. If he responds with a list of sizes and prices, then you can make your first counteroffer.
   b. If he asks you to make an offer, respectfully ask him to provide a starting number. It's always best to have the seller make the first offer—if he refuses, offer Stock X payout to get a better idea of where their number is.

3. Once he has given you his starting price, you can make a counteroffer.
   a. If you're close to his number, say something along the lines of "Could you come down to _____?"
   b. If you're far off from his number, say something along the lines of "We might be too far off, but I've been paying _____ for pairs—I would be at _____ for all. Let me know if you can come down." Make it clear that you understand that the seller needs to make their money as well. This will make you appear more personable and increase the likelihood of the seller coming back to you in the future.

4. After giving your counteroffer, wait for his response.
   a. If he rejects your offer, ask him what his best price would be.
   b. If he counters your offer, send another offer yourself to get a better price.
   c. If he accepts your offer, you can move forward with the *logistics* of the deal (payment, shipment, etc.). If you're paying well (close to Stock X ask), have the seller pay for shipping. However, if you're paying under market, offer to cover shipping—don't get too greedy.
5. After negotiation, decide if the deal is worth it for you.
   a. If there is not enough value for you, respectfully thank him for his time and pass on the offer.

Personal Example

Jordan 1 Obsidian: After doing my research, I decided to purchase over 100 pairs of the Obsidian 1s in January of 2020. After making a WTB post in some Facebook groups, I was quickly connected with a local seller who had around 20 grade school pairs for sale. He was asking $200 for grade school sizes, but I offered $160 per pair to minimize my buy-in cost. He initially declined this offer as he wanted to look for someone who would pay his asking price. I temporarily walked away from the deal but made sure to check back in with him the next week. He still had not found a buyer who would pay his number, so I knew he would be more likely to take my offer. I reminded him of my initial offer, leveraging the fact that he had not been able to sell them yet, and he quickly agreed to run the deal at $170 per. After meeting up with him, I made sure to double check and legit check each pair before bringing them over to my storage unit. I sourced another 70 pairs in men's sizes from a store on the East Coast around the same time. I ended up buying them all at an average of $260 per pair. At this point, I had 90 pairs—but I still wanted more—so I posted another WTB in a Facebook Group called Banned LA, and bought another 30 pairs in both grade school and men's sizes. Because many of the sellers weren't local to me, I made sure to pay through PayPal Invoice so that I was protected as a buyer. I then legit checked everything and brought them to my storage unit where they sat for around six months, until prices hit $500+ in every size. I then reached out to one of my bulk buyers who I had made a strong connection with over the years. We agreed on a price of $500 per pair—and since he was local, he came to me and paid full in cash. After everything, I made around $240–$300 per pair, leaving me with a total profit of over $30,000.

Connections

As true with most things in life, it's not about what you know—it's about who you know. The value that strong connections can bring you is limitless, so emphasize building good relationships, no matter with whom.

People reach out to me every day asking how to find a bulk seller/buyer, and how to start a relationship. I always recommend getting involved with the reselling community on both Instagram, Twitter, and most importantly, Facebook. Start to follow/join sneaker accounts/groups and interact with their posts. Eventually, you will be able to pick out some of the major bulk players in the game. From there, you can form a relationship by simply starting a conversation, or something that I find works the best, buying from them or selling to them. This doesn't mean you have to buy 100 pairs right off the bat, but sometimes just buying a single pair, whether you want the shoe or not, is enough to get your foot in the door. You must understand that most bulk sellers do not have the time to talk to people who they aren't doing business with. Thus, by making any type of purchase, it puts you ahead of the other people trying to get in touch with them. Once you've started your relationship, you can move on to inquiring about bulk.

As you continue to do business with people, you will start to build a reputation. It's up to you as to what that reputation is; so, make sure to always act professionally. I'd hope this would go without saying, but never let your emotions take control of your actions, and always honor your word. In this business, where we're buying and selling generally with people we've never met, your word is everything. The easiest way to lose a connection and hurt your reputation is by flaking on a deal.

I do 80% of my bulk buys with the same select sellers. I've built strong relationships with these individuals through consistent business, respectful negotiation, and sticking to my word. As a result of treating my sellers well, they treat me well—offering better prices as well as offering me bulk before anyone else. Once they offer bulk, don't be afraid to counter their price, but don't offer so low as to offend them. Doing so could lead to you losing that connection and opportunity entirely. If you can't agree on a price, simply thank them for their time and move on. I've seen far too many relationships be broken simply because people don't know how to carry themselves in a respectful manner.

Never expect somebody to return a favor to you, but always return a favor to them.

Examples: Earlier in the year, I purchased over 225 pairs of Jordan 1's from a seller. This seller was connected himself, so I knew I wanted to make a good impression. We closed the deal smoothly, and after word spread that I am an easy to work with, cash-ready, bulk buyer, that same seller's bulk provider ended up reaching out to me, asking if I was interested in purchasing more bulk at a discounted rate. I quickly established a strong relationship with this new seller, consistently spending money with him. Just recently, I bought 122 pairs of the Jordan 1 "Mocha" from him, paying $305 per. At the time, it was almost impossible to find bulk at this price—I was only able to do so because of the connections I had built. I had previously hoped to buy-in at $280 a pair, so when I was offered bulk at $330 per, I wanted to talk the seller down. I was confident that the seller would negotiate on his price because at the time, the market seemed unpredictable, so people were hesitant to hold their pairs. Since then, Mocha 1's have risen to $470 per pair, giving me a profit of around $18,000 just a couple weeks after I bought in. I reached out to the same buyer who purchased my Obsidian 1's and asked if he was interested. He initially offered $450 per pair, but I was able to talk him up to my price of $470. Again, he came to me and was able to pay full in cash, avoiding any transfer and shipping fees that we would've faced if he wasn't local.

payment email to you, trying to get you to ship the shoes to them. The reason for overnight shipping is to cut down the chances of you realizing the scam and rerouting the package.

"Multiple Owners on One Account"—while there are legit joint accounts, I've seen too many people get scammed from accounts with multiple owners. These accounts can build up lots of references quickly as they have multiple people doing business. However, with most of these accounts, the other owners will not take any responsibility if another owner ends up scamming somebody, so there's just more risk when dealing with these accounts.

"No mutual friends"—this only comes into play when you've been doing business on Instagram for a while. If you're well connected in the community with reputable people, the chances of not having any mutual friends is low; so, stay away from accounts like these unless you can pay through GUA.

Payment

Paypal—PayPal offers a couple ways of paying: "Gifted/Friends and Family" or "Invoice/Goods and Services." When you pay through friends and family, you opt out of any buyer protection. However, there are no upfront fees on the transaction. This is something you can use when dealing with a trustworthy, reputable seller. For goods and services, you have buyer protection as long as you are detailed in describing what you're purchasing in the invoice, or the payment note. Always make sure to include that you're purchasing brand new 100% authentic shoes with original everything. If they insist on having you pay through friends and family, make sure not to use your balance but rather, use your bank so that you can always fallback on their protection.

Bank Wire/Zelle—This way of paying offers you the least amount of protection, so only use these payment methods when you trust the seller 100%. Generally, you won't be able to make any claims on this type of transfers because of all the verification steps you have to take before sending money this way. This is typically the preferred way of receiving payment for sellers.

Venmo/Cashapp—These payment methods also offer you little protection, so again only use them when you trust the seller. It is easier to get your money back if you get in contact with your bank, but obviously this is something you want to avoid happening.

Gifted upon arrival (GUA)—This is the ideal way of paying for sneakers but is only viable when you yourself have built a reputation as a legit buyer/seller. Essentially, the seller will send you the shoes first, and you pay once you have received them and legit checked everything. You have complete protection when buying this way. To stay organized, ask the seller to include a slip with their info inside the package.

Legit Checking

The longer you're in the game, the better you will be at recognizing fake sneakers. However, if you're newer to shoes, there are plenty of resources available to help you authenticate pairs. If you live near a sneaker shop, many of them will do free legit checks for you—just go in and ask if they can help you out. Online, there are groups where you can ask for advice, as well as apps that legit check sneakers for a small fee. When trying to legit check things yourself, something to invest in is a black light. Certain materials will react differently to the light, so you can compare how your pair reacts to a legit pair. Also, some fakes will have a factory stamp on them, which can only be seen with a black light. The Stock X tag itself reacts to a blacklight a certain way, so you can even check the authenticity of the tag. There are also many YouTube videos that you can watch that look specifically at the "tells" of a certain shoe.

CHAPTER 8

HOW LONG TO HOLD

Before investing in a sneaker, you can establish an estimate for how long you want to hold your shoes. However, as a sneaker starts to rise or decrease in value, you have to be able to recognize when you should start to sell pairs.

First, if your estimated hold time is around 6 months, and the shoe has not moved in value after the predicted time has passed, you may want to consider selling your pairs and investing into a different sneaker. Oftentimes if a sneaker goes down in value, investors don't want to sell their pairs because doing so realizes the fact that they lost money. However, it is better to reinvest that money, even if it means taking a small loss. You don't want to get stuck with a shoe that won't go up in value because you are too stubborn to accept a loss. There's a term in stocks called a "stop-loss," which is designed to limit loss in a certain position. When a certain position hits a certain number, the trader or the software will automatically sell. You can apply a similar principle in sneakers. Have your own "stop-loss" price in mind and force yourself to sell if pairs drop down to that number. However, don't be afraid of a temporary dip when investing long-term. If your plan was to hold a shoe for over a year, don't be afraid of a small dip at the three-month mark.

On the other hand, if your investment was successful, and you have seen growth in the hold, there are a couple of strategies you can use to determine the optimal time to sell.

To start off, a base rule to go off is that if you start to see a plateau in price growth, sell as soon as possible. Oftentimes in the sneaker market a plateau will last around 3–4 months before prices start to move again, so it's best to sell at the start of that period rather than wait out the 3–4 months. You can reinvest that money into a different shoe, hold for 6 months, and then actually buy back into the shoe that had plateaued. For example, the Jordan 4 "Cactus Jack" rose from $400 to $1,000 in under six months. This was the best time to sell. Prices ended up dropping down to around $650 for three months, before eventually taking another three months to rise back up.

When deciding whether to continue to hold or sell, ask yourself if you would invest in that specific shoe if you had the cash right then. If not, consider selling. However, because sneakers are an actual product that takes time to both buy and sell, you must factor in handling time to your decision. For example, if you had invested into 100 pairs of the Jordan

1 "Smoke Grey," and decided that if you had that money in cash right then, you would choose to invest into a sneaker other than the Smoke Grey 1's, you have to also consider whether it would be worth it to sell all 100 pairs of Smoke Grey's and buy a high quantity of that other shoe. It's not as easy as stocks/options where you can trade all on a computer in a matter of seconds. You may decide that it makes more sense for you to keep holding the Smoke Grey 1's, even if that other shoe would have a slightly higher return.

CHAPTER 9

SELLING

Where you choose to sell depends heavily on how many pairs you have, as well as how quickly you want to move them. In this chapter, we will cover the pros and cons of different selling platforms to help you decide which works best for you.

1. StockX/Goat: These platforms have really established themselves as major players in the game because of the ease in which you can sell sneakers with them. You simply accept or wait for a bid, ship the shoes to get authenticated, and then get paid. However, you pay for this simplicity through seller fees, which means you end up getting around 10–15% less than what the bid/ask was. This option is great if you don't want to have to worry about making sales or waiting for your shoes to sell—you can just click a button and get your payout within a couple

days. However, if you are looking to maximize your profits, you should look elsewhere. You also must consider the fact that this way of selling will take up the most time as well as force you to deal with other expenses like tape and boxes.

2. Consignment: Everyone has heard of big-name shoe stores like Flight Club and Stadium Goods. If you pay attention to the sneaker world, you would know that these stores are known for their extremely high prices. For this reason, most resellers ignore these shops. But, somebody has to supply these stores—so why not us? First, I'm sure some of you are wondering what exactly consignment entails. Consignment is when consignors (us) send our shoes into shops like Stadium Goods, Flight Club, or other local stores, and let them sell the shoes for us. Once the shoes sell, the stores send us our money after taking their cut (usually around 10-20%). The profitability of consigning comes from the difference in consumer bases between platforms. The people buying shoes on Flight Club are not price-conscious shoppers—they want their shoes fast and are willing to pay however much Flight Club is charging. Thus, even with the 20% fees, you can usually end up making much more than you would on a platform like Stock X. The major con to this method is that you have to wait for the store you are consigning at to sell your shoes before you get paid. So, if you want your money quickly, you may want to sell somewhere else. Something you can do if you have a high quantity of pairs

is send a size run to each of the different major consignment shops to increase the number of potential buyers. See which stores are moving your pairs the best, and then continue sending pairs into that shop.

3. Social Media (Singles): Selling through social media eliminates the seller fees, and allows you to make the sales yourself. By selling pairs individually, you can target people who are looking to purchase pairs for their own personal use—this type of customer is usually willing to pay well. You can maximize your profits this way, but you also have to deal with making the sale yourself, which includes negotiation, communications, as well as packaging and handling the shoes yourself. This way of selling is best if you have a lower quantity of pairs or have very strong clientele. However, it can get tough to manage if you are trying to sell a high quantity of pairs individually.

4. Social Media (Bulk): This way of selling can be the quickest and easiest way of selling your shoes in high quantities. You can find a buyer using connections that you have made or the same concepts used in the "Where to Buy" chapter. Private buyers as well as bigger stores are almost always willing to cash you out for the right price. If you can develop a strong relationship with a private bulk buyer (which is what I have done), you'll end up with a great option for moving any and all pairs you want to sell. You can also go ask your local sneaker stores if

they are buying—oftentimes they can pay fair if you can offer a good quantity of sneakers. While this is the quickest way to move your inventory, you also have to expect a lower number per pair. Generally you'll have to sell pairs for around $20 less than what you could get per pair individually.

CHAPTER 10

REINVESTING

After selling off pairs from an investment, it's important that you put that money back into another sneaker. However, while it's easy to rush into a new hold with exaggerated confidence after a successful investment, you need to take some time to reflect on your last hold and determine what your realistic goals are for future holds.

Look back at your last investment—if it was successful, really try to understand why. Did you follow past trends or look at the colorblocking and prices? Did any influencers wear the shoes? If so, how did that impact the market? How long did you have to hold the sneakers? Could you have bought-in later or did you time it perfectly? Learn what worked well for you, and try to apply those same principals in the future. If your last investment was unsuccessful, why was it not? Was the shoe unwearable? Was there not enough visibility? Was there too much stock in comparison to the demand? Were there too many other investors holding the same sneaker? Were you too impatient—did you rush into the hold or did you sell too early? Recognize where you went wrong and learn how to avoid the same mistakes in the future.

Once you have reflected on the past, you can start to look towards the future, with more experience, and hopefully more capital to work with. Use the same process as before, while making adjustments to what you found worked well for you. Have patience before buying-in again—it is better to let your money sit until you find a promising investment than to rush into a hold that won't actually make you money.

CHAPTER 11
LOGISTICS

This chapter will cover some of the logistics you must consider when investing into sneakers, including storage, shipping, spreadsheets, and taxes.

Storage

As long as you're dealing with a manageable number of shoes, try to store your shoes at your residence. However, if the quantity becomes too high, or you find yourself tempted to sell off your investments, you may want to look into investing into a storage unit. This is something that you can write-off in your taxes, and use to get some extra space or an extra step you have to take to access your inventory. For some people, it's worth the money just so they don't have to constantly see the shoes they have. The more accessible the inventory, the easier it is to cave in and liquidate your pairs. There are generally two types of storage units: outdoor or indoor. While outdoor units are easier to access, I would recommend getting an indoor unit just for added protection. When purchasing your storage unit, try not to specify that you're keeping sneakers there—just say it's old furniture or sentimental items. There have been unfortunate cases of workers at storage unit facilities taking items from units, so it's always ideal to take extra measures to protect yourself.

Unit Size	Average Cost (Monthly)	Maximum Capacity	Realistic Capacity
5' by 5' by 10'	$60	680 pairs	150 pairs
5' by 10' by 10'	$90	1371 pairs	300 pairs
10' by 10' by 10'	$140	2742 pairs	600 pairs
10' by 15' by 10'	$170	4114 pairs	900 pairs

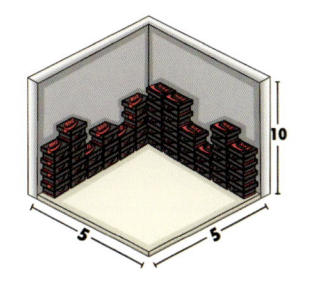

Logistics

Average Cost: $60
Maximum Capacity: 680 pairs
Realistic Capacity: 150 pairs

Average Cost: $90
Maximum Capacity: 1371 pairs
Realistic Capacity: 600 pairs

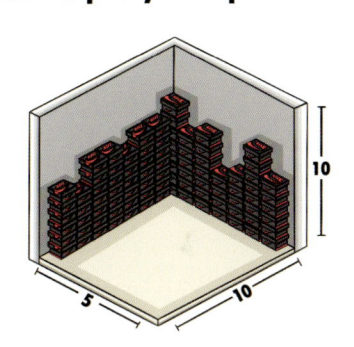

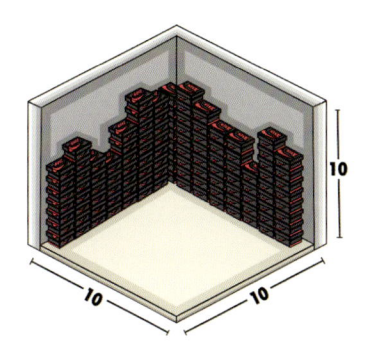

Average Cost: $140
Maximum Capacity: 2742 pairs
Realistic Capacity: 600 pairs

Average Cost: $170
Maximum Capacity: 4114 pairs
Realistic Capacity: 900 pairs

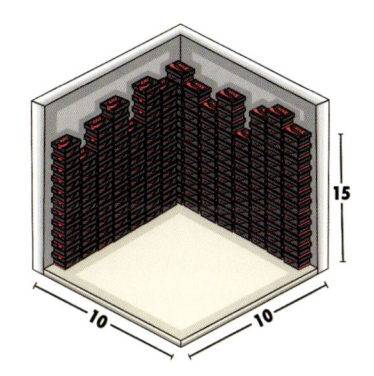

Shipping

When buying shoes, it's generally ideal to make sure the seller is responsible for the package until you receive it. This eliminates your risk of the package getting damaged or lost. When selling, make it clear that you are not responsible for any damage to the package, and that insurance can be provided upon request. This way, you are protected from any mistakes by shipping companies. Before creating your label, you have to figure out the dimensions/weight of the box you're using. You can find boxes at stores like Staples, Home Depot, and Lowe's. After putting your shoes in the boxes, fill any empty space with anything to reduce movement within the package. Then you can compare the prices of the major shipping companies (USPS, UPS, Fedex) to determine which you want to use. Keep in mind that shipping speed can be impacted by external factors. For example, USPS was backed up around the time of the election due to the prioritized mail-in ballots and is always backed up around the holidays. You can check shipping rates directly from the suppliers, but there are also other platforms that offer label services. These include sites like Pirateship, Shippo, and Paypal. When you're ready to drop off your packages, just head to your local drop-off location—with larger packages, it's always recommended that you get a receipt/proof of shipment, even if that means you have to wait in a longer line.

Logistics

Spreadsheets

Keeping good records of your business is crucial to managing your investments as well as filing your taxes. You can get more detailed if you choose, but there are a few main components that I think are essential to any spreadsheet:

#	SHOE NAME	STYLE NAME	DATE PURCHASED	PRICE PAID	PRICE SOLD (AFTER FEES)	PROFIT	DATE SOLD	ROI	TIME SPENT
1	OFF WHITE UNC	JORDAN 1 OW	APRIL 2019	$20,000	$40,000	$20,000	AUGUST 2019	200%	4 MONTHS
2	TRAVIS SCOTT	JORDAN 4	APRIL 2019	$30,000	$50,000	$20,000	FEBRUARY 2021	166%	22 MONTHS
3	SBB 3.0	JORDAN 1	DECEMBER 2019	$12,000	$24,000	$12,000	FEBRUARY 2021	200%	14 MONTHS
4	CONCORD	JORDAN 11	APRIL 2019	$8,000	$15,000	$7,000	JANUARY 2020	188%	9 MONTHS
5	LEGEND BLUE	JORDAN 11	FEBRUARY 2019	$6,000	$12,000	$6,000	DECEMBER 2019	200%	10 MONTHS
6	PINE GREEN	JORDAN 1	AUGUST 2020	$50,000	$60,000	$10,000	FEBRUARY 2021	120%	6 MONTHS
7	ROYAL TOE	JORDAN 1	JULY 2020	$17,000	$32,000	$15,000	DECEMBER 2020	188%	5 MONTHS
8	DARK MOCHA	JORDAN 1	NOVEMBER 2020	$30,000	$48,000	$18,000	MARCH 2021	160%	4 MONTHS

Shoe Name:

Style Code:

Date Purchased:

Price Paid:

Price Sold For (after fees):

Profit:

Date Sold:

ROI:

Time Spent:

 These parts can make keeping track of inventory much more manageable, as well as filing taxes. You can also study your spreadsheet to see what worked best for you, and what didn't work well.

Taxes

Note: We are not a CPA—we're merely offering advice which you can take at your own risk.

The most important purpose for your spreadsheet is to help with your taxes. Without it, you would not be able to calculate and declare your profits, meaning you would be taxed on your total gross sales. Payment companies and the IRS don't care about money spent unless you have clear records of what it was spent on. If you're a casual investor, there's no real need to open up an S-Corp or LLC, but if you start to take it seriously, and are moving significant numbers, I would advise you to register as a corporation. Doing so allows you to write-off certain costs as business expenses. This includes things like the cost of storage, gas money spent transporting sneakers, or any other fees of running your business. If you get to the point where you are really moving weight, or if you have any other questions regarding taxes, I recommend you hire or reach out to your own tax accountant/financial advisor.

CHAPTER 12

CONCLUSION

By now, you should have a strong understanding of how to invest into the sneaker market, and more importantly, you should understand the process of what goes into any similar investment. It's my hope that the specific principals in this book can be applied to other markets, specifically clothing, whether that's Supreme, Off-White, or any other popular brand. You should be aware of the factors that impact a shoe's potential, the best places to buy and sell, as well as the optimal times to do so. As I'm writing this, I've actually just liquidated some of my holds, realizing profits of over $200,000. As evidenced by my success, these methods do work; however, in order to see growth and success yourself, you must put in the work. Go back and reread this book, making sure that you truly understand each and every chapter. Don't skip over the case studies, and don't ignore any one part. Each chapter has been carefully selected and then crafted to aid you in your investment journey. Take the knowledge that you've gained and start to apply it. You can use the information given as a guide for future releases. Take risks, gain experience, and reflect. Only by doing so will you be able to master *The Art of the Hold*.